Why I Decided To Stop ?

About Racism

Table of Contents

Full list of chapters

Why I Decided To Stop Thinking About Racism

- *Chapter 1: **Prologue***

Asher Sommer. Born in 1978 is a German Ghanaian Entrepreneur living in China.

We are living in special times. A time where not everything is making sense anymore. Where new words can be created and filled with a whole lot of baggage. These words will circulate in all types of mass media until everybody believes this is real. Except for that all the stations have been playing the exact same message over and over again, many of these words are nothing but empty shells. The problem is the conflict these things bring us, the damage it puts into friendships and other relationships. This will not be talked about. I started writing in blogs about this topic, when I was deleted from an African

German Facebook group. The reason. I was cancelled by the group for doing the following.

A member posted, all the members should start to keep distance from their white relatives. Since they are white they have been profiting from black people's presence for too long. Further she said, this includes the ones who are nice to us or act to be on our side.

The crime I committed. I dared to oppose her views. I said just because some people here are close to "Black Lives Matters" I will not cancel my white family members. Family is family. Why should we use racism against whites to fight racism? Where does it make sense?

I expected some verbal attacks against me, the typical discussions about me being a sellout or traitor. I already expected something like this. But there was silence. Then I checked my activity log and everything has been deleted. I was kicked out from the group.

So here I am. I am probably the result of Dr. Martin Luther King's dream. I am half black half white. I live in China and my wife is Chinese. I was an unofficial member of the African German music group "Brother's Keepers". I was also the founder of the African Atheist movement. I was always working on ending racism. My goal was a life where we all can live together without one group fighting the other. It seems like that the political industrial complex is not interested in that. Instead they weaponize people. Divide and conquer the population. So when nobody speaks to each other, people are less likely to come together to protest against their policies. It's amazing how they are able to twist this idea as if they are actually using the division of people to sell us the story as if they fight racism and intolerance.

The only reason why they can go ahead with that is because the people are sleeping.

I felt I have to write this book to bring back some common sense. I am aware that people will push this into the right winger category. I don't care. I am neither right wing nor leftist. They are both the same. Hateful people. I am a freethinker. I cherish freedom. My choice will always be freedom over totalitarianism. I have travelled the whole world and I can report from an incredibly wide angle. I am able to speak multiple languages and I can read many more including those of Chinese and Japanese script. I have friends from all different cultures in this world. I have friends from all sexual orientations.

I am not a divider, I always united people.

I have been a businessman for over 25 years. Especially in business race doesn't matter.

My success in business came from being open and inclusive. Reliability and respect are what really counts, nothing else.

Even if you are skeptical this might not be the right book for you, because you have heard some negative comments about it, give it a try. Read it to the end and if you still disagree, please leave a comment on my website. I am very excited about the feedback.

Why I Decided To Stop Thinking About Racism

- *Chapter 2:* **Racism In School Explained**

So when looking back at my childhood, there were many
incidents of racism which I encountered. From today's
perspective, were they really of a racist nature? Maybe the
motives were some totally different ones. So let's dig into this.
I grew up in a village in Germany. At that time the population
was just 2000 people. The place was close to the highway to
Hamburg, so a lot of commuters settled there to be able to
afford a house instead of living in an apartment inside the city.
At that time we had about 20 kids for each age group, which is
a very tiny number. I was born in 1978 , so I was born at the
time with the lowest birthrate. So here we are. The first day in
school. A group of kids from all different backgrounds. I was
not just the only non white kid. I was the only black kid and as
well the only kid who had a totally different pronunciation of

the German language, the only kid with a parent from Africa and the only kid from a farmer background. So at that time we were just kids. Very soon I became the subject of bullying. I was beaten by classmates all the time, as well as by kids from the 3 grades above us. So what made me become the target? I was the one who was clearly different from everybody else. Another factor I need to add is, I was also the second youngest in my class. I turned 6 years old in May. With the exception of one other boy I was the youngest.

So in school the typical groups were forming just within the first 2 weeks. In sports class people would soon find out who is best at sports. We had 2 girls groups. One was the girls who believed they were pretty. The other group was the not so pretty girls. The boys had the sports guys; another group were those, that were closer geographically so to speak. They were pretty much neighbors, some even knew of each other before school started. Then you had the boys with spectacles, the fat boy and the ugly one. These were the ones I had to be extra careful of. I later explain why.

Just like anywhere in life, when people get together. They quickly form groups and they quickly go together with people they believe they have the most in common with. So I was the outsider. On the surface I did not have anything in common with anybody there. When I talked, others would laugh. So I became careful to talk to people. Probably quiet. Teachers would correct me if I said something and the grammar was incorrect. Something which was even more of a weird factor, I did not share the same religion with the others. At that time I was a Mormon. I was also not allowed to bring friends home if they were not Mormons. For my own part I decided not speak about it. The first year I went into several brawls and after the first six month were over, I understood that I must fight back in order to defend myself. I always came home with bruises and my mother told me to pray to god. That didn't help. Then she said to hold the left cheek if they hurt the right one. It also failed. One day a classmate was punching me on a wintery day, I was already bleeding. He was the strongest in our class. Also the oldest. I then saw he was standing on a frozen sewage drain. I punched him. He slipped and I straight attacked. From that moment on I was respected. Over the time in primary school and also when attending secondary schools I always went along with the same strategy. Go and find the strongest guy. Knock him out whenever there is a large crowd and then none of the others would touch me.

So my question, was this racism? Did the other kids who bullied me just did it because I was black? Or did I become a case of the hierarchy?

What do I mean by hierarchy?

As I explained, there are the kids who know each other long before school. There are kids who are neighbors. And there are kids who are wearing eyeglasses or might be ugly looking. This is what I mean by hierarchy. The strongest or fittest will be on top. Everybody else will be below them. Anybody will do anything to not become part of the bottom quarter. Once you are there, all the other groups will not look at you. Defending their position means ignoring those who come below. I'm looking at a greater scale into our global kindergarten society. Even for adults nothing changes. Nobody with an OK paying job wants to go one step down the ladder. With this in mind, the kids know their position. They will fight for it. If there is somebody who does not fit into the pattern, they will make sure he comes behind them. Right on the bottom.

This is the same pattern in any competitive society. But also in communism there are ranks.

First come the party officials, then party members. On the bottom. Non party members and "antisocial" people. The more important a good standing in the society is the more extreme the hierarchy.

So since everybody wanted me to take a seat on the bottom, I basically had to look out for attacks from all sides. I then noticed that the people, the closer they themselves were to the bottom the more aggressive they became. The ugly boy and the fat boy were just looking for an opportunity to strike at me. Then in the second grade one of my neighbors joined the school. The only person he knew was me. So mission one. Strike me as bad as possible so he could set himself apart from me. Then he started terrorizing others and made it quickly to the top in our class. He was quite good at sports and he fitted into the pattern of the image which was popular at that time. He was tall, had blonde hair and blue eyes. Since that was all he could offer he knew very well to promote these features. So he called me out, because I was the opposite.

At that time the boy was supposed to be my best friend. But I always had him in mind as the blueprint of a racist.

During my entire time in primary school and also later we always used to clash.

In a way, I needed him. He was always the prototype of a Neo Nazi for me. He was the living form of an ongoing oppression against me.

What I did not realize then. There were so many other factors in the equation.

In fact this guy was very jealous.

He was maybe the only person out of my class who visited me at home. He was living close by.

The house his parents lived in was not fully paid. His brother was handicapped and the family was actually struggling financially. I on the other hand came from a farm. Our house was huge. Our land was even larger. This was normal for me, because I grew up there. It was just not normal for others. Just because I was not aware of that I was the kid who had abundance at home, this guy saw my unawareness as a weakness and made sure I would always stay one level below him. He came up with rumors about me. He was fighting me with ideology. There was a time when we were playing outside and they would pick names like Hitler or Mussolini for themselves and I was not allowed to play in their league. I was excluded from the sports teams and so I became the goalie during soccer training. Nobody wanted to be the goalie. So I somehow had my peace. It was a no competition.

Another big factor. The parents. My time in primary school was during the mid 80s. Black people were not that popular with older Germans. The topic of Africans having HIV was all over the news media. As I wrote earlier many of the people living in our village left the city to live a more comfortable life. A big role in it played the fact that in the inner cities a lot of schools were already crowded with foreigners. Village schools offered the luxury to have only German speaking children. This was a big plus. Even though I was the only black guy. I was not the only mixed child in my school. There were several other kids who were half Spanish. Fortunately they were not as visible as I was. You could not see Spanish written on their face. So they all decided not to talk about it. They would not attack me, but they would simply ignore me while we were at school. None of them would have thought about helping me, when I was in trouble.

So back here. The last thing would have been that I would visit other classmates in their homes. Many of the parents would not really be in favor of that. The first 2 years I did not really visit classmates. On my side I was also not allowed to do so. If I wanted to see them, the Mormons would tell me that I must bring them to the church. I then had most of my friends outside of my classmates. Something I kept on doing later in my school time.

Anyhow by grade 3, I started visiting friends. I also had a better bicycle and so I went to see classmates. That was the time when I experienced that I was not too welcome in their homes.

Looking back from a later perspective. It was not racism. These were usually middle class people who were struggling to build their families. They were not interested in having extra baggage. They didn't want to tell their kids why they did not want me around. They were just as the ugly kids in school trying to defend their position. Make sure that people they see as inferior stay one level below them. They did not care about giving people a chance.

They were not interested in my character; they were not interested in my history. They just saw dark skin so they totally blanked me out.

If encountering people from a richer background they acted a lot different. They would ask questions. They would be interested in getting to know me. But here I was probably the person that was blocking the interaction. In my personal view, they were all the same to me.

I also understand now that those richer people were not in a social struggle with me being an outsider. They didn't need to care what others think about them, so they were open for a conversation.

During that time it was all obvious racism to me and I started hating myself for who I was. I didn't want to be the outsider. I wanted to blend in. I was not like them. I lived different, I had a strange name. Probably even a stranger family. Out of all these factors I saw racism as the main problem.

I even kept defending this issue later, when I was thinking about people in other schools. I was kind of an inner conflict. Witnessing reality, but still sticking with old beliefs or pain from unhealed wounds. I later saw Turkish kids in school terrorizing German students. In Germany the secondary schools are divided into 3 levels. The high level called "Gymnasium", which has nothing to do with a sports gym. Then there is the "Realschule" This is the medium level and ends with the 10th grade. The low level school is called "Hauptschule". This type of school ends with the 9th grade.

Afterwards the students need to start work. Usually it's the foreigners attending the low level type of school. Mostly kids come from Turkey, from families who don't speak German at home. When attending such schools, in some places the German kids who attend such schools are in the minority. The majority bullies them for not being able to speak Turkish. They bully these kids for not being Muslims. Many Turkish kids will use these German classmates to let off steam for their social anger.

In such a situation, are we still speaking about racism? If we look into at the media and how people report about this, it's rarely ever mentioned. In case it will be discussed they will always call it as an incident of personal differences.

I can agree to a certain extend. But what is missing here is an honest debate. It is not racism. It's still about the hierarchy. It will always be the same picture. Everybody wants to be on top or at least be part of the majority. Everybody who fails to get their entrance into one of these groups will fight against the others who also did not get a chance to fit in.

This is the main struggle I see in every society. I have seen it all over the world. The closer to the bottom the fiercer is the competition. The more likely it is someone will use physical violence. Look at what happens in the inner cities in the USA where kids sell drugs. They are on the bottom of society. They will kill each other rather than going home empty handed. This goes for men and women. Women are less likely to have physical altercations; still they will play social games to shame their opponents. In a group of girls, attention is the currency. The girl who gets the most attention will take the lead. Every other girl who is able to get along with her will be part of the main group. Those who get no attention from outside will be totally excluded from this group. Those girls will form their own group. But don't think there will be peace among them. They will show a certain amount of decency towards each other. But that is only masquerade. Each one of them is ready to fall into the back of the next girl. Still they understand they must act as if they get along. None of them wants to be entirely lonely.

Once you are completely lonely you are what I consider the outsider. The outsider will never be accepted into any unpopular group unless he or she is totally surrendering to them. For the popular group, the outsider does not exist. They see no need in any interaction with people who are not part of their group. So the only way for outsiders to get contacts lies outside the own group or school class. Usually the outsider will search for potential allies with similar interests. Be it music, video games, drugs, religion, race or fetishes.

If the gay person in the class does not find other gay people in the same class, the person will automatically become an outsider. The person then has no choice but finding other gays outside they can interact with. Only when that happens maybe one or 2 other people in the same class will tolerate the person. But nobody wants to interact with a 100% disliked person.

When I attended secondary school, I was not a popular guy. I was again an outsider. This time I was in the low level category part outsider. 2 other unpopular guys used to be my friends. When the other 2 guys changed school I was back to be only by myself. I then went out and joined the most respected gang in town. The gang that everybody heard about, but none of them would be able to join. The gang, which name alone would get some serious attention. Me and my best friend at that time joined. My best friend was also an outsider. He was from a different school.

Once my classmates knew I was in the gang, they all heard about and did not dare to think about joining, the respect towards me was totally different. I was still an outsider. But I was the cool outsider. I never participated in any class meetings. I never went out with my classmates for lunch break. I always went out and met my other guys from that so called gang. This is when Hip-Hop started in Germany and we were the weirdoes. We dressed different, we walked different. Everything we did was totally in stark contrast to what my classmates did.

In my own life this was a point when I totally left the community of my class. I then did a sophomore year at the same school. Changed classes. Still even after being welcomed with open arms. I just skipped that and continued the subculture life. It was the first real escape from society for me and I totally enjoyed it. School was school. My spare time was my spare time.

When our gang broke apart, and I exited my old group, because we all delved into a drug lifestyle, which I quit when the others became too serious about it. I was again alone. I was the outsider to my classmates and an outsider to the cool people. That's when I got together with some of the greatest people I've ever met. They were all outsiders, we came from background of all walks of life. And here I finally found home.

We were all freaks. The mission, be the loudest freaks in town. It didn't take long after we made serious waves and became a very popular crew.

What I'm trying to say by that. There are different ways to treat the outsider's role.

For some people being disliked and alienated is something negative. It also brings all reasons with it to just give up. This type of passiveness would lead to staying at home to become an overall introvert. Then these introverts will let their own family deal with the problem. On the surface it's not their own fault, so they force themselves on parents and family members. People they can fall back on. This is probably a lot easier. In that case you might find a school psychologist who will confirm the situation, so that the parents must accept this as given.

The other way to turn the existence as an outsider into something positive is a lot harder. I was somehow forced into that because of the struggles I had in my family. There was no foundation to fall back onto. So instead of going from A to B and back, I tried a lot of other letters in the alphabet. By doing this I was able to experience a lot of different characters from those people I was around with in school. By doing that I was becoming more flexible. Since my character also had a lot of features others didn't have I was also quite interesting for others.

During those times I probably learned a lot about myself and my character. I was not shy of taking challenges, because whatever I had at home was far worse than what could go wrong during the time I was hanging out with other interesting people.

To make a point here. It took me 3 decades to see this clearly. The main issue was not my skin color. I will explain it in a different chapter. The issue was that I didn't fit in into the hierarchy.

There were others despite them having black skin color; they found it way easier to fit in.

In later generations with the upcoming popularity of black people in sports and music the picture was even more likely to be upside down. Everybody wanted to be the black kid's friend. Everybody wanted to be seen with somebody who might look like the current biggest superstars.

This means the formers losers in their hierarchy games are now the winners. Still there might be others who lose instead. This time we might see kids with red hair who are being alienated. It might not have anything to do with color itself, or with anything I just mentioned. It might be that the kid with bad computer skills is now the kid to be ignored by others. There are always different reasons that make up the hierarchy. I have seen the sports guys being replaced by young musicians. Then the drug dealers had their time to rule those groups. Times are changing, but as odd as it may sound. The hierarchy always exists. It seems to be a constant of nature. Just like planets orbiting a star.

Why I Decided To Stop Thinking About Racism

- *Chapter 3:* ***Jobs And Business***

So when we start our career, get our first jobs. How is the process working?

We write an application to several companies and hope to be contacted for an interview.

During the interview we are showing ourselves from our best side in order to get the job.

Only a small number of people will be able to get the job. Most applicants will go home with a notice the company will call them back.

So let's look at it from the other side. The company needs to hire new talent for the job positions they need to fill. The pressure is on the recruiters to find the best possible person to fill the seats. They are given a general guideline what kind of people each department is looking for. And not only this. There will be a list of preferences the company has, because these types of people who fit into that pattern have been proven to be successful in the last rounds the company was hiring. Here the judgment is quite pragmatic. The company's success depends on finding the right personnel. Anybody who is not performing according to requirements is a financial loss.

So when it comes to the assessment of applications, who will be sorted out first? Anybody without the fitting academic skills first. This will already account for a very large percentage. Couldn't we label it as a selection? Even racism based on skills? Ah ok, and next is of course selection according to prejudices. They will check people with equal credentials according to their living situation, their family status and also according to their racial background. You hear the bell ringing? According to racial background!

Why is this? First when you hire a person from the racial majority the amount of trouble you might have is considerably less. The person will be able to speak the language, will have fewer problems to fit in with the colleagues. Probably lives in the same neighborhood than the other workers. All these things are important. Especially for a startup, where tensions inside the company could mean a huge loss in performance.

So this means if there are no regulations, the person of color must offer some more striking benefits in order to be picked by the recruiters.

What is supposed to be suppressed in the general public is a huge factor during the process of hiring workers. Any type of prejudice will automatically become part of the process. The person who looks like a drunkard will be selected out. The people who come to the interview and slightly look tired will be selected out. The people who are too confident might as well need to go. It's also not always welcomed when you have people who might lecture the boss. Nobody wants that. So the fat people, the recruiters might have gotten a memo should be only very few. They got an idea about how many candidates should be women. They will certainly look at information such as if the woman is newly married and could get pregnant within the next few months. She could be on a paid leave as soon as she starts her job. These are all factors which have to be taken into consideration. The management needs to be sure the company will be competitive. If they themselves make mistakes during hiring, this could often mean the competitor will surpass them in a short time. Business does not wait for anybody. What we see here is a very natural selection process.

I have to break it down to make it look a bit more simple. You want a team of soccer players. You will have to look for the best possible players you can get. You have to check their record where they played before, where they scored best and also if they have been loyal to their previous teams or they have been just opportunists. Here for the sports of soccer, race will less be an issue. But when looking at basketball. As a non black player you chances to be selected are very unlikely. I'm still waiting for the first Indian NBA player. It will probably never happen.

This is where I want to make my point. When hiring programmers it is an established fact that Indian coders are preferred over let's say white Americans living in a trailer park. So the chance for an Indian person from Bangaluru to be drafted by an IT startup is much higher than for an American who just happens to be white. So it is an established prejudice that Indians are good at programming. This time the prejudice goes in favor of a different racial group. Nobody out of that group will complain. But the white programmer will not be so happy about it. In that case he must deliver when he fights for his position.

The Indian guys on the other hand will probably have a hard

time to be drafted as security guys, Here the advantage and I repeat it's because of prejudices is on the side of black males. An Asian woman would also have no chance to get hired as security guard unless she is 6 foot tall, weights 100 kg and is a martial arts expert at the same time. Otherwise no chance. So where are Asian women petitioning to become truck drivers? It will not happen. What is called a prejudice is also the usability. Those who have the biggest muscle financially will be able to pick the best candidates. The ones without the proper finances will have to take the ones that are left over. Here it would be the chance for the candidates to perform well. As long as they can prove an excellent record they can also land a job at a better company later. It just doesn't come without putting in a certain amount of work. So if you are naturally bringing the right genetics or you are blessed with an extraordinary skill set or you might be an overall genius. Of course you will find the means to prove it. But unless you were not able to show and prove, you remain Mr. Nobody. There will be a need for any type of person in the job market. Unfortunately this includes also jobs which are not that popular.

So if not getting the desired position. Somebody will have to fight their way up the ladder.

This for sure will be hard, but at least there is a way.

If somebody wants to still sneak into a position which is hard to get for them, the best chance is to do an internship. With a good performance here the company will understand that they need the person, so the chance is given to land a job. Another way is to offer a deal. Tell them to start work for a lower salary. It must make sense for the employer as well.

In any business. Either you deliver exactly what is required or you must sell yourself under price. In order to get into a business deal, the other side must see an advantage. A loss cannot be accepted. At the end of the day it's all about the numbers.

There are reasons while in certain business fields the salaries for women might be lower. In others again the salaries might be higher for women. It's a matter of the usability.

There are jobs a black person might have to be satisfied to earn less. There are also professions where a white person has little chance to get into. We must be honest that some of the prejudices have a lot of truth in them and are often based on common sense.

Like in Africa where the Chinese construction companies bring their own workers rather than hiring locals. There is a reason for that. When I was about to finish school and was supposed to apply for a job, I was complaining about racism before during the hiring process. I avoided it altogether by starting my own business. Here I had to work at least twice as hard, but I didn't need to go through the typical working situation. When I then had to start hiring people I saw the importance of proper judgment. I had a clothing store. Here I must be sure the sales person is able to sell. Somebody without any talent for sales will ruin the performance. Also I became aware that not everybody is trustworthy to take care of the cashier. So again, it may start from bias. But when you don't exercise proper judgment in business you will trust the wrong people. By doing this your company will close down as soon as it opened. I also had my time in managing events. It all comes down to the same rules. If you are too tolerant with your workers, you hire people who are not professional. The chance you get enormous setbacks is very high. I could probably find numerous examples what happens if you work with the wrong people. I saw club owners who had security guys opening their own cashier. Alcoholics working at a bar who drank more than the guests and still required their salary. It then doesn't take long until the plug is being pulled. If those people would have used common sense, they would have been probably a bit more prejudiced by assessing the usability of the workers. They could have easily guessed what could happen.

When the guy managing the wardrobe makes more turnover selling cocaine than the entire club, something is wrong. When you run a clothing factory and the workers are sewing too slow. There is a problem. Unless that problem has not been identified and changed by its root, the only consequence is bankruptcy.

I used to be in favor of affirmative action. After some years passed I would only suggest such measures should be placed upon larger corporations. For small businesses it is an unnecessary burden. Any type of quota will only distort the performance.

The job market is an open competition the same way as sports. When every black runner would need to carry an extra 5kg weight around each ankle just to give people of other races better chances, it would also not make any chance. Or let's say every white basketball player will get a double score rule for every point landed. This would destroy the game. Like I wrote before, there is always a field somebody has a clear advantage, and for those they don't, there is still a chance to show and prove.

What is also important, once a person has gotten a job. Inside the company the same rules apply as in school. The hierarchy will be also in place. The group which is the majority will take the lead. All others will have to find their position. Again here those who don't fit in will face a tough competition from coworkers. Unlike in school, where only the individual score matters, here different departments must produce a common result. When one person inside the chain does not perform satisfactory, all others will have to struggle or make up for the lost performance. This will create tensions. The better workers will file applications to other companies, while the lower level workers will openly start attacking the person who constantly makes the projects fail. What bosses in that case are extra careful about? Imagine this is a black person. The chances are high the black person will go out in public by claiming that the company treated him bad because of race. The media will welcome the person with open arms. This is a bad publicity not every company can afford. This might be another reason when for example companies hire Indian workers. First of all they would not be in the spotlight by the media. Then they would be able to form entire groups, where their own people would know how to manage that person. In case if the person is really not working, they will handle this situation the Indian way. So the boss may not need to become involved personally at all. In some cases when a black person must be hired, the owners of the company would even need to create a position for the black worker where he or she cannot easily be attacked by coworkers. So after all it even makes black people less attractive in the job market. Especially when the black lives matters topics were all over TV. Sure certain people were able to let off steam. But generally finding a job for black people was a tough job. Especially in professional fields. Who wants to hire a person who might subject to publicly complain over bad treatment at the workplace?

My message might be a bit controversial for many readers here. I think I made my point.

The situation on the job market should not be regulated. There will never be a solution which would satisfy everybody to the very end. The job market as any type of business is an ever changing environment. Today's requirements will not be in demand in the coming years. In business nothing is ever steady. So this is why regulation already doesn't make any sense. Whoever wants to join the job market must show they have what is in demand. Here race doesn't play a too big role. If it were all about privileged white people, who don't want to share they space with non whites. Asian people as well as black people would have no chance in the job market. The opposite is the case. People from Asia have even a higher chance to land a Job than whites. In almost any field. It's not because of how they look. It's because they are hard working. They value a good job more than African Americans and they see the long term bigger picture. Even the Mexican who does most low level manual labor jobs understands that.

They all don't get blinded by the racial divide. This is why they will win on a long term perspective. The Mexicans will overtake the African Americans in numbers of population and in income very soon. The black people will also lose their political power.

Why I Decided To Stop Thinking About Racism

*- Chapter 4: **Africa***

If you believe you are a black activist, never go to Africa.
Never.

Why did most black so called activist never go to the
motherland? All these conscious rappers, speakers and authors.
Many have never made it there. Or just South Africa, which
has almost nothing in common with the rest of the continent.
So in 1997 when I was on my first trip to Ghana I was still in
my Malcolm X mindset. I travelled together with my white
father. It was on the last day of 1997, an amazing year. I started
my own business, while I was still in school. So going to
Ghana was interesting and a challenge for me at the same time.
Apart from my father no white man was there to blame.
Everybody from the judge to the janitor was black. The first

thing I noticed. Ghana was not a country of poverty as I learned in school. The people were relatively happy. Life was very slow motion. A place like Accra was a buzzing city. They had more tall buildings than I saw in Hamburg. Germany is usually still unchanged from its medieval structure. I have been to New York the years before, which of course was the total opposite of Germany. Ghana of course did not have anything comparable.

What was perhaps most striking was how the people reacted towards me. When I entered Ghana I was no longer a black guy. I was a lot whiter here. So when going to Africa, this is interesting. People there like to be white. The whiter the better! Many women would use bleaching crème to make their skin tone look fairer. Many people would say they admire white people for their intelligence and their ability to create order. Most people were not interested into gangsta rap as I was. A more British gentleman way of life was far more popular there. Even people who would listen to Jamaican Reggae music and are deep into Rasta culture would still listen to Westlife or Take That. The young people there were not what I would call pro black activists at all. Of course if you are looking for such specifically, you could find them. But are they 100% serious? I doubt it. And why should they. They have other things to do. Youth unemployment is very high. Many people just live on their own family's welfare. A lot of people have at least one family member who is living abroad. Either England, USA or Germany. Based on that, the families share a certain level of development. Those who have a relative in the US usually receive a lot of money from that family member. Either though trading goods or direct payments to them. They would boast wearing American fashion and having typical American haircuts. Then there are those with family members in Britain. Here it was mostly about education. Everybody would bring one relative over for studies in college, so they can bring back an academic degree when coming home to Ghana. Those would dress in proper British looking outfits, giving an appearance in a way resembling more a Carlton Banks style than a Will Smith like attire. These people would have the largest influence in society. They are mostly those who are the best educated ones. Or at least act as if they were. Another group would be those with relatives in Germany. Here they would wait decades for their family members to come home. Just when the person comes home, he or she would generally come with lots of money, an expensive watch and have

pictures ready of their cars they drive in Germany. Everybody

knows Germany is known for good cars. It's every Ghanaian's

dream to own a Mercedes Benz. What they don't see is often

the hardships these family members go through while staying

abroad. They don't know how hard it is to even get a working

permission in Germany. Additionally, whenever they think

about going to university all of their previous education is not

being recognized. As a result of that most people will end up as

low level workers in German cities. Especially Taxi drivers.

For at least 10 years they will not make enough money to even

sustain their own lives. This does not stop them from going

back to Ghana later and brag about how much money they

have earned. The cars they show in the pictures, they mostly

don't own them. The watches they are wearing are usually

rented. Rented from somebody in Ghana, who owns the

watches. Usually Ghanaians underestimate the seriousness of

German bureaucracy. There is nothing comparable to German

bureaucracy anywhere in the world. Still this does not stop

them from trying to chase their luck abroad. The same story

will repeat again and again.

I remember I was often stopped on the road and asked by those people where I come from. When I said Germany, some people would tell me to come to their house and then they would straight ask if I can send them an invitation letter. I then always asked them, what do you believe you will be doing in Germany? One guy said maybe become a doctor or a professor. I told him, there are zero professors at that time from Ghana in Germany. Without a proper education the educational system there will be ignoring you. So then they still insisted in getting my address. I then just walked out.

That time I already thought it is irresponsible to be bragging about the good life abroad. Knowing too many people who got there usually faced never ending times in misery. I remembered all the people I saw in my uncle's Afro shop in a West German city. Everyday people were only gathering with their countrymen. Drinking Guinness beer, watching football and talking Ghanaian politics. A too familiar picture. Most of them don't have work or just help out as a janitor once in a while. The money they earn can hardly sustain a life in Europe. Maybe out of 20 people one person will be able to become successful. Usually that person will be quick to learn the language and then just take the jobs, they are given and work themselves up the ladder. This means they need to learn to work as hard as Germans. When coming from Ghana this is a huge challenge.

Every time going to Ghana you can see how everything moves slowly. The average speed cannot be compared to big cities in USA, Asia or Europe. Everybody is easy going. People will sleep at work. Then resume at a slow pace. This continued until in 2010 more and more Chinese laborers came into the country to build new roads. The Ghanaians are blaming everything from the weather to the mosquitoes for their slow performance. But then the Chinese did not seem to have any of the same problems. In summer the weather in China is usually much hotter than in most parts of Africa. The mosquitoes are also more. So the Chinese will be even happy to work in a much milder climate. With upcoming competition from abroad, the Ghanaian workers, over the past decade, switched up in gears. And all of a sudden entire projects have been able to finish.

All of a sudden entire roads have been paved. A lot of missing infrastructure has now been completed. Many built by Chinese. Others have now also been completed by Ghanaian firms. Just before the Chinese came, it was not the main issue that money was not available. People were just too lazy to move anything. They would request payments for work they have never completed. Corruption wherever people were looking. One of the biggest economic factors in Africa is churches. They are responsible that there is never any foundation of wealth being laid in Ghana. When staying in Ghana for a longer time. It's easy to see that most families live for their Sundays. This is when they all meet in church. During the week they will wear old rags or even second hand clothing. But on Sundays all that disappears and everybody will wear custom tailored suits. The women will wear their best most elegant dresses. They will spend the entire day on Saturdays only for making their hair. A church culture, only comparable to the likewise in the United States. The big difference is the amount these people will pay in tithes. The pastor will read how much everybody contributed. Nobody wants to fall short in payments. Ghanaians believe in paying tithes will contribute to better fortune for the week to come. So they pay as much they can. Often people will deposit their entire incomes to the ministry. Nobody will pay less on tithes than the general average amount. If doing this, those people will lose their face. There are even people who go to church every day of the week. They will pay a lot more.

Just by this happening, the churches will make so much money that every Monday they will transfer the money to their Swiss bank accounts. By doing so every week the cedi currency drops for another round. Like this there has never been stability in the monetary system. The politicians have always been cutting the zeroes. But anybody with a brain would save their money in foreign currency. Whoever doesn't have savings will spend all they have by end of the week. Next week the value would be less anyway. These churches have been the cancer of the country's economy, but they are controlling public opinion. Any attempt by a politician to end this, has failed since. The pastors hand in hand with the corruption are what has been the sand in the engine of the economy Ghana could have been. The biggest problem I see is that the people are way too religious. Ghanaians and also the populations in neighboring countries are all very serious about religion. Instead of making plans how to solve the many problems they have, they will turn to god in a prayer and then hope for a miracle. Some problems as simple as that the roof has a hole will not be fixed for years. The person will pray for a decade to god to fix the problem. And even when the house breaks down it will be valued as a sign from god. The prayers have been answered. By being religious, the people never learn to take responsibility of their own lives. They always wait for others to help them out, on a smaller and on a larger scale. The politicians all over Africa show a common image. They beg for financial aid from outside. They will never roll up their sleeves and start working on the problems by themselves. The countries definitely have the manpower. The major problem here, it is close to impossible to move people. Those who could work always feel entitled to get more. Many people have the attitude that they should get rich from the first job they do or better not work at all. It is also no help that most people who are rich are actually pastors. And these people only work for one day every week. People therefore have the idea that rich people are not working at all. Only people work who are living in the remote countryside, because they are too poor and then they have no other choice. In general people are all very religious. They have multiple Christian congregations. On the other hand there are also areas in every country with a group of Muslims. In Ghana that is in particular in the north of the country. For those people it's a similar way of life. Their only duty is to pray to Allah. Whatever else happens is god's will.

So as weird as this example might be. Somebody has been

praying in the morning. Asking god for a large amount of money. As always. Then in the same very day the person is filling in for a coworker to sell vegetables. Somebody comes over and buys all the vegetables. The person will see the payment as a sign from god. Put the money in the pockets and tells the coworker later that the vegetables were stolen. It's so common that the people would twist and turn the stories in a way that the prophecy is becoming self-fulfilling.

It is also very common when helping people out in Africa, there will not be any thanks after the person has gotten what they wanted. In their books they already prayed to god. You helping out only means god has done his job. This is something I have very often talked about with relatives.

If I didn't mention this, they might have never thought about it in this sense.

I have often played with the idea, what if the state would close all the churches. Are foreign imported religions the root of all misery? Are these used as tools to mentally enslave the people? Is everybody a victim only? I did my research. Of course it is the common mechanism to give foreign aid, so that the money can be back to whoever granted the funds has it back within a short time. The banks and corporations know that this is a way to make the countries dependent on foreign goods. As long as their own economy doesn't produce the same goods they will have to import those. Generally most consumer goods in Africa are imported. Apart from mainly agricultural products, printed fabrics and raw materials such as cocoa, metals like gold and bauxite. There is also oil available. Still in general the productivity is very low. Africa is the richest continent in natural resources. Unfortunately the minds do not exist locally to understand what to do with any of this wealth and abundance. This explains why the brain drain is happening. Further on it's the religion, where people only wait for miracles. They simply don't see the need to act. So what would happen to them if the foreign religions would be taken out? For this the explanation is simple. People would resort to natural religions. Superstition on which ideas like voodoo are based on, would become the base of their believes. The outcome would not be that different. Just through organized religion, the people are easier to control by outsiders. Just if a voodoo priest would be able to collect tithes for himself, he would still transfer the money to Switzerland. All that would not change.

Then laziness is another factor which seems impossible to solve. I personally think Ghana is an amazing country so rich in resources and full of great people. On the same side it's the mindset of the people that stands in their way to achieve better. This lets unfortunately all the well educated people flee their country. They all believe they must go abroad to become successful. And it has proven them right. The most intelligent Ghanaians are now in USA and the United Kingdom, not in Accra or Kumasi.

This brain drain is still going on. The education system in Ghana is still lagging behind. People rather steal the funds than complete building the schools which are needed to prepare the younger generations for the future. Of course somebody may argue the money which is spent for education only benefits European nations. Surely, but there have been many decades since Ghana has become independent. Still there has not been any significant improvement, so that intelligent people would keep staying in Ghana and use their brain power in their own country. As far as I look I cannot find the evil white man anywhere to be the problem in this equation.

Most public schools in Ghana are run by churches. Instead of a proper education in math and natural sciences, the focus is on language and especially on the bible. One might argue it's the fault of the churches. In fact they only do what benefits themselves. They create a population that will focus on paying their tithes. That's all. There are also schools by European fundraisers. These are valued actually as the better schools. Still these schools have the focus on raising funds in Europe from old people who believe their form of charity matters. After they removed all their own service fees, the money which reaches they schools in Africa is just enough to hire photographers and child actors to make more photos of starving children.

The problem would be. If the churches wouldn't build schools, the corrupt governments would not do the job by themselves. The politicians are too busy enjoying the money rather than taking action. Most of them themselves have been to private schools abroad. So they have no idea about what is actually happening in their own country.

Not everything is bad as well. Ghana has the longest political stability of any country in that region. They have less tribal conflicts than let's say Nigeria. There are very few weaponized conflicts inside the country. The whole place is generally very safe.

I'm still sorry to say that, but the problems which were huge problems when I was a kid, 40 years later still haven't been solved.

I believe also in 100 years Ghana will not be "Wakanda" as shown in the Marvel/Disney movies.

And this is where many theories I put together myself are based on.

Every society in the world was prepared for bad times. Like war or famine. Only the people living in West Africa were never prepared for anything. When the colonial forces from outside came. Small countries like Portugal arrived first. They could just take whatever they wanted. Then other countries came. Denmark started its first trading colonial post in Christiansbourg Accra. Then the British came and setup their own posts. Had the people been better prepared they would have been able to defend themselves. Unfortunately Africans are good at anything but planning long term. A plan is only a reaction as a result of catastrophe, which has already happened. Nobody would plan ahead for months and years to even out all eventualities of an impending event.

This is what the Europeans are masters in. Since the weather has 4 seasons every year. By fall the harvest must be in. Whoever fails to collect the harvest will not make it through winter. It's a life or death scenario. In Africa there are no seasons. Just months with dry climate and others with humid climate. Basically the weather is very steady. So nobody needs to plan ahead. Nobody is in need of making big dramatic changes or reactions. There were always fights between tribes, but none that would last for decades. Europe prior to colonialism has been at war nonstop. Later their wars would be fought on the sea or in the colonies. In Africa it would be nomadic tribes fighting local settlers. Robbing them of their belongings. Even slavery was very common all over Africa prior to the European influence. There were slaves sold to Arabs centuries before the roman Vatican legalized the practice of slavery. Black eunuch slaves were spread all over Asia. Especially along the silk road. Even in China there are statues showing Black eunuch slaves in statues. We made the discovery in an old building in Hangzhou China. Muslim Sheiks have been using African Guards for their harems. They did not allow their slaves to procreate, meaning they were always castrated. This is why we don't find any African settlements in Turkey, Iran or Pakistan. Their ancestry ended with their lives as slaves. Often the African slaves became figures in popular history in all those places over Asia, they were just not able to create any offspring.

In a way we must still thank the Europeans to handle slavery in a more humane way.

I leave it here with my comments about slavery. This topic just shows the insanity of humans. I will, not blame a particular group of people anymore to be responsible for the international slave trade.

What I still need to mention is the inner African slavery. It was very common if one tribe battled another, the victorious tribe would enslave the members of the losing side until they were fully assimilated.

On other trips to Africa I went to places like Ethiopia. I also made a stop in Nigeria once.

From what I observed, the differences between single countries in Africa are also very great. East Africa is an entirely different culture than any West African country. South Africans are again totally different from western Africans. The reason Africa is the second largest continent after Asia. It's also not as small as depicted in our maps. Alone South Africa, Botswana and Namibia together are as large as the United States without Alaska. Congo and Angola are also huge countries. So even when black people meet outside of Africa we are always greeting each other and form communities. We often don't see that each of our countries is totally different from the other. While Ghana is very relaxed, people in Nigeria can be aggressive. It is impossible when even bringing 2 Nigerians of opposing tribes into the same room and expect them to treat each other friendly. The people of African Arabic countries would always look down on non Muslim Africans, even if those are richer or more successful than they are.

So when staying in a place like Hong Kong, people from most African countries would great each other. It's a common practice the diasporean Africans are doing all over the world. But once people from Sudan or Somalia enter, they will not great anybody. Especially, when the place has a Muslim majority. I especially noticed this in Dubai.

Then there are slight differences between French speaking countries and former British colonies. French speakers will stick with other French speakers. English speakers will dwell among themselves. So places like Senegal and Ivory Coast will have something in common from French rule over their countries. Meanwhile Kenya and Ghana had British rule, so they both have an English setup.

The total difference would be northern African countries. Here the population is actually not African. The name Africa itself comes from the Roman emperors. The world was named after the Roman provinces. During the rule of Caesar, the province opposite of the Mediterranean Sea, opposite of Rome would be called Africa. Which is today's Tunisia. When the Germans finally conquered Rome, many people fled Italy for the southern provinces. So these are the populations of Morocco, Tunisia and Algeria up to today's Egypt. Most of those people pride themselves for not being black. They are all Muslim and have more in common with the Spanish than with Cameroonians or Nigerians.

So last but not least there is the view of the black Muslims in the US. They seem to believe there is an historical united Muslim Africa. They call it the Moorish empire. I often wonder why we don't hear much about it in our history. We understand that African Americans do not know any of the African history, but still they have a lot of legends in circulation which do not add up with what we learn in Africa. Of course the Moors were existing. But the majority were Romans who converted to Islam. They were active in Tunisia Morocco and Mauretania. At a time they were also expanding into Spain. The caliphate of

Andalusia is probably the best researched one. Unlike the Nation Of Islam wants to make people believe. The moors did not rule over all of Europe. They were not black. They were just darker than the later northern Spanish who are mixed with French and Germans.

This is why they were referred to as brown. Upon further research they were not related to the many African tribes, such as Songhai, Wolof, Mandinka or others. Even the Berber of Morocco, were totally black before and resisted Islam for centuries.

For the other tribes Islam was a way of trade. My own tribe the Ashanti used to be Muslim before we came to Ghana, but we abolished Islam, when the religion became stricter with the teaching of the Quran. A real orthodox Muslim lifestyle is very much un-African.

To sum it right up here. To go to Africa and to expect to find out that racism is the cause for all evil makes no sense. Especially as an outsider you must first of all find the right part of Africa you believe you are belonging to. Then you will realize that many of the problems which existed outside of Africa also exist on the inside. We always like to romanticize certain things we don't have sufficient knowledge and experience of. We do this because we know we might never be able to see these places in our lifetime. But once you are there. You find out that your problems still exist, then you should check the root of these problems somewhere else. Maybe within yourself.

I remember one story when I was in Ghana at the Airport. I brought my brother to the main entrance. This was the trip, when my brother sand I had brought my father's body to Accra for the funeral. My brother and I both have long hair. In Ghana we would be called Rasta. Even though we don't listen to reggae music or associate ourselves as Rastafarians. The guards at the Airport were very rough. I just helped my brother with his luggage and the guard went in between. Closed the door and did not let me say good bye to him. I then told the guy with a weapon in hand I just want to see him before he leaves. He then pushed me away. The guy was 1.85 tall, with a statue of a gorilla. So I called him a gorilla. I said do you think because you look like a gorilla you can push me around? The guy went crazy and started beating me down. This reminded me of a situation I would also face with security guards in

Germany. So no matter where you are, it's always the people with the same type of mindset becoming police officers. It has nothing to do with color at all. And I would always be seen as a disturbant. Somebody who dares to question the authority of their badge. So I had my trouble with custom officers in Ghana before. For them I was automatically a drug addict because I have long hair. They forced me to open my luggage during each visit to search for drugs. Even then I did not make the connection. The problem has never been my skin color. It's the personality that I have and how I express myself in general. The last time I experienced that to the extreme was in an Airport in Chennai India, where I was detained by a military police officer pointing a machine gun to my head. They put me in the basement and interrogated me for half an hour.

They were unable to see that I'm not Indian. And they were angry because I dared to make trouble at the airport, after they denied me entry because my mobile phone had no power. So I was unable to show the itinerary of my ticket.

Why I Decided To Stop Thinking About Racism

- Chapter 5: ***African Americans Vs. Africans***

This is a very sensitive topic. It's very easy to offend somebody. This is why I write about it.

If you are a very emotional person, you are free to skip to the next chapter.

There are many points to talk about African Americans and Africans. Especially in the USA there are often rivalries between Africans and African Americans.

Then there are Caribbean people who are somehow standing in between.

The whole thing starts with African Americans expressing their discontent with white America.

Always stressing the negative sides of the American experience. This is something outsiders can hardly relate to. So while the music videos are also available in Africa. Videos which are coming from American musicians, showing how rappers mock police and other authorities. How they use gun violence and graphic language to show how they are killing other black people. Using swear words and profanity at every chance. This is something every person from Africa would call very un-African. And in fact there is nobody in Africa calling each other the "N-Word". People would use these words to describe African Americans in some parts of the continent.

Africans on one side don't understand slavery and the experience as such. That there are generations existing in USA without a history of their own. Also most people in Africa don't see white people as a big problem. Just in hotspots like South Africa where the black population has been going through Apartheid for several decades. In places like Kenya there are thousands of white people living together with black people and there are no incidents of clashes between races over there.

Then we have Africans who make it to America. In a way they have the same level of ambition as people coming from India or Pakistan. They do not come to America to live like African Americans. They want to live like white Americans. For many years they will play the green card lottery or enroll in overseas study programs to become accepted by American universities. Once they are successful, they will leave everything behind and come over. They probably have several family members who collected money for the tickets. As soon as the person gets a job he must promise to pay the money back. So then totally convinced this is a once in a lifetime opportunity the person will go. Once arrived, they will see the disparity between rich and poor. But unlike for the African Americans this disparity is nothing new. In Africa the wealth gap is even wider. And most of the people immigrating to the United States are not coming from a low level background. They just feel they are wasting their time in Africa. In their mind it's not racism holding them back. It's Africa.

So while they get accustomed to the new place they will feel thrilled by how quick everything is working. How fast the services are responding. How people can make big moves in a very short time. Remember from the last chapter. In Africa life is slow. So then going to job interviews, they see that they are very welcomed by recruiters. The recruiters are happy to have a black person in front of them without the usual "chip on my shoulder" attitude. The gentleman personality doesn't feel fake, like it's only something the person needs to act like to be able to get the job. The person might not get one or two jokes during a meeting, but everybody can see this person is honestly motivated. So not only will the African person be able to prove their abilities. It's also a chance to grow in the career. Especially as American companies like to send their workers to further their education and enable them to attend seminars. Expect the African worker not to miss out on one of them. So fast forward a few years. The same person will be in a very steady situation, with a nice house in the suburbs, enjoying all the benefits America has to offer. So now they come across some African Americans and these people will start talking behind this person's back. What kind of sellout is this? He is more on the side of the white boss than on the side of other black people. They don't realize, if they cut out the negativity, they could have achieved the same position. So the African Americans quickly get offended when the African person acts as if they are joking when they tell him or her about how much the system is designed to impose institutionalized racism. This is the word.

In fact the African person will have no clue what these people are talking about. Didn't he or she just perfect the American dream in a short period of 4 years? Then these guys come in and act as if this is impossible for them? They claim the system is holding them back?

The African person will then start to investigate. They will go and look at the schools. They will see that the average public school looks 20 times better than anything they were using in Africa. It couldn't be the education. The school has all the necessary equipment. If this person in Africa had this equipment, he or she would have probably been able to complete the studies in half of the time. So the next argument would be the bad neighborhood. It takes a trip to the other side of town. They people live in smaller houses. The roads are not that good. But compared with what the average people have in Africa it's still 50x better. There are no open drains. No holes in the roof. They all have clean sanitation. A house with a modern kitchen. It can't be the neighborhood's fault. Then somebody might take the person around. They will be shown pictures of slavery. About how segregation was affecting the people. About how people didn't have equal rights. Once this happens the person might start thinking something really bad happened to African Americans. But then looking at what year it is. It's been a good 50 years since the civil rights movement. And even before that. Most states did not have enforced segregation. In all states slavery ended after the civil war. Places like the New England states never participated in slavery.

So how come young people, born generations after segregation still seem to suffer from these events? This is where both sides won't find a common ground to touch base."Usually when the African immigrant later gets married to an African American wife they will get soaked into these ever occurring episodes of racism. When they instead chose their partner from an African country, this drama will only begin with their kids.

All of a sudden you will see African kids feeling they have been enslaved by white people. In the chapter about the role of the media I get into this topic in depth.

Theoretically if the kids would not get exposed to the same media, all this brainwash would not sink in so deep. If the Immigrants are of Indian or Pakistani origin, they would not be affected at all. They don't have a weapon called the media directly targeted at them.

Is this because of racism? I would argue no. The Indian community in the US is too small to play a significant role as an economic factor. This is why.

It's not a secret that even in China people know that the African Americans are a huge block of consumers in the United States. There is probably a whole city in China where they produce fake plastic hair for African American women. They all know who the biggest spenders are.

It is a tool by the industry to keep the African American people in a state of self unawareness. If they would wake up and understand they do not face any limits, their consumer behavior would be affected. A good example is a company like Nike. The Nike Company knows at the first of the month, their earnings from all types of basketball shoes are safe. Nobody spends as much money as African Americans on shoes. If they would not like their product anymore Nike would go bankrupt in a very short time. If African Americans would not buy Nike shoes, who would make up for those losses? White people in general don't buy sports shoes for over 200$.

So as consumers, African Americans have a lot of leverage over the US economy.

Then let's have a look at African Americans. What are the similarities with Africans, while we have already looked into the differences?

African Americans came basically with the second wave of slaves. Originally slavery was legalized by the Roman Catholic Church. It was the Portuguese who started shipping people from their colonies to their newly gained territories in South America. This all happened several decades After Christopher Columbus discovered America for the Kingdom of Portugal. Then The Spanish who had the bigger fleet of ship also started to get into the race for colonies. So a good way for the Portuguese to develop their new property was to bring slaves. So the first round of slaves were Angolans who were shipped to Brazil. At that time both countries were connected by the Catholic Church via the Vatican. The then pope legalized slavery and the competition began. After Brazil was already taken by Portugal, the Spanish Invaded one country after another. Columbia, Argentina. The Portuguese then tried to secure the colonies they already had, The Spanish then were quicker and started taking slaves from West Africa. The distance between Angola and Brazil is too far, so going in from Mauretania made more sense. When the Portuguese started doing the same, they captured slaves from Capo Verde. The French started to join the race.

They went into Senegal, Then also Ivory Coast and shipped the slaves from there to Louisiana. Once the French started the British couldn't be backseat spectators anymore. They knew if they let the French go ahead they will also lose their power in Europe. The British already established colonies in New England, as well as further south in Philadelphia and the Carolinas. Meanwhile the Spanish took Texas and Florida. While the Spanish took more slaves from Sierra Leone West Africa, the British first took over former Portuguese ports like Lagos in Nigeria. They also set up a post in Ghana and Liberia. Then they started shipping people from those places to the areas closer to the French and Spanish colonies. In the case of countries like Togo, almost the entire population of that country was shipped to America via the slave castles in Ghana and Benin. This is why I would claim the majority of African Americans originally came from Togo.

African Americans are physically typical West Africans. They have the same physical features as West Africans. Some people who are able to distinct tribal features can very well classify where a particular face originally came from. In Africa there are huge differences between appearances among various tribes. The slave race between the colonial powers on one hand ended with the battle of Trafalgar. Here the Spanish were significantly beaten by the British, who then retreated from most North American colonies. New developments in weapons technology enabled the British to come out as the winners. But their reign did not last very long. The French then experienced their revolution, so they also had to withdraw from some of their territory to Canada. The colonies of Louisiana and Florida were taken by British colonialists.

In return the New England states started to revolt. Soon America became its own Nation. The British then only kept control over Canada. Also took over the French territory. The Spanish were beaten in Texas and retreated to Mexico. Out of what was remaining The United States of America was born. From 1776 to 1890, there has officially been slavery within the United States as a country. Whatever happened before was happening because of the colonials powers, who were fighting over the territory. Still I also mentioned this before; In the New England States slavery was forbidden. Slavery was something happening in the confederacy. The people who owned the slaves were not the Irish Americans living next doors. As many black people would just randomly accuse any white person of profiting from slavery, many Irish also came to America as slaves. Just in the very beginning when the Spanish started using African slaves for their territory the British thought they would just use Irish to do the same work. It just wasn't that successful of an idea. In the southern confederated states, the Irish couldn't compete with the African slaves. So they were also starting to use African slaves. So many people are asking who were the slave masters? Many people would come up that the names which were given to the slaves reveals who their owners were. This is false. When slaves were baptized they would adopt an English name. The same thing happened in Africa, when early missionaries were established. People who were baptized then chose a European family name. So who were the slave masters? The answer. The same people who still lead the industry. Whether it is food, tobacco, cotton. Basically all the landowners who later founded the corporations. The people who were the main round of investors into all kinds of banks. They were the ones with the capital. They used to have ranches as large as entire cities. For example Washington DC use to be the land owned by the first president George Washington himself. And of course he owned slaves. It does not make any sense to blame it all on white immigrants from Europe who settled in the US during World War 1 to be responsible for slavery. It does not make sense to blame polish Americans or German Americans for slavery. Those were the people who were traditionally always against such treatments. It was even the European philosophers who condemned slavery and they were very vocal in what later resulted in its abolishment. People like Albert Schweitzer were just few, who were engaged in changing such malpractice. There was no such movement in the Spanish or Portuguese world that would encourage the same. So giving the white northern Europeans the whole blame for slavery is an especially cowardly act from all the Roman Catholic nations. They have been starting the race. Just because they lost it does not free them from guilt. And then there is another question? Who were the shippers and the traders? A chapter, which in today's brainwashed society, I'm unable to discuss on a broader scale. For all the time slavery happened. There were white people helping the slaves to escape. There were people in the northern states who gave the runaway slaves their citizen status. Surely there were extremely insane white people instrumental in organizing slavery. No doubt about that. But to claim all white people are inherently evil, does not do white people any justice. Then we have the industry. The corporations, directed by the people behind the curtain, who are exactly those who profited from slavery, nowadays donating money to organizations such as black lives matters, just to draw attention to where it does not belong to.

Especially in a context where politicians increase prison terms. Invest into the industrial prison complex. Which is run again by the same people who profited from slavery in the very beginning. Then come out publicly, point the fingers at those who did not have any connection to slavery. Call them racists because they are simply patriots who love their country and then use the media and associate them with the results of the laws they enacted to make an extra buck from prison labor. It is pathetic. This is also no critique of capitalism. The people I am looking at now are communists, when it works for them better, they are capitalists when they can also profit from that. They are the establishment, they have always been the establishment and they will do anything to defend their position. There is no doubt about that slavery was wrong.

We Africans love our brothers and sisters in America. They are part of us. Africa will always be your home.

I hope every African American who reads this message sees the chance I offer here. The problem is not racism. The American dream can be yours if you give America a chance. Like president Trump said "What do you have to lose".

There are incredible African American Achievements. No other group of people has been able to create what is called American culture. American Music culture would not be all over the world without the amazing African American contributions. The way to innovatively recreate, reimaging entire concepts of music, is something we have not seen anywhere in this world. The many contributions to art. To science. Today's America without those African Americans who have been working hard, to push the boundaries would not be the same. Without the brave African American soldiers who were fighting in World war one and two. America would not exist in the same way it does today.

I'm very sure there is no white person who would deny these incredible contributions African Americans have made to the society.

I think people should understand what advantage this is. The great diversity America has to offer.

And a last word to the media industrial complex. If you only focus on everything negative in the culture, don't expect that people do not see what is happening. It's all about division. It's the media that puts the microphone in the hands of extremists, so these people can be used to increase the bias. Why do the media only show stupid black entertainers acting completely uncivilized? As if there are no intelligent black people available to produce music and entertainment. It's because they don't want this. They don't want the people to unite. It cuts into their profits. Not into ours.

Why I Decided To Stop Thinking About Racism

- Chapter 6: **President Obama**

For many decades black people in the United States believed that once a black president makes it into the white house, things are going to become better. It has been an ever repeating call all over the media. Black people talking about black presidents. Hoping for a black president. Waiting for a black leader. This was something which was always discussed in the media since Dr. Martin Luther King's speech in front of the Washington capitol, so that even people all over the world anticipated it. In the late 80s Jesse Jackson became a candidate in the political race for the democrats and since then people believed that somebody like him could stand for a better way of doing politics. Fast forward to the 90s Bill Clinton was praised to be the "cool" President who a lot of people would claim he could act like a black man once in a while. Of course that was part of his campaign strategy. Still a lot of people bought it. So it manifested in their minds that the blackest a president could get, would be a white man like Bill Clinton. A man, who is not black himself but seems to be very familiar with black culture. This was also used when Al Gore was running against George W. Bush. People believed Al Gore to be the more suitable candidate. Since people projected similar qualities into him, as the former president he served as a vice president. The bigger was the disappointment when George W. Bush took the election instead. A lot of people were devastated in their hope towards a better world. This devastation was probably even felt more around the world than in the US, where many people better understood who Al Gore really is. Then 9/11 happened. After that Al Gore was kind of forgotten. The country was on alert ever since. Terror was the main topic in any media and in almost any discussion.

The results, the United States attacked any country that was accused of having ties with the terror attacks. Under George W. Bush the US war budget was raised from 250 Billion to over 1 Trillion dollars. This was the rise of people who expressed their doubts. Movies like Fahrenheit 9/11 surfaced where

Michael Moore asked many questions, which should have been asked. The truther movement was born. People started questioning 9/11 and the events which lead to the attacks. People started to question parts of the narrative. This went as far as that for many people saw the connection between the Bush family and their choices where the next wars are going to happen. People started using the internet to express their anger. When it came to the elections in 2004 still nobody believed a lifeless looking John Kerry would be the answer to all that which is going wrong. People rather didn't vote at all than they were voting for Kerry, so lucky Bush was able to run the show for another 4 years. 4 more years of unnecessary wars and obvious corruption. A lot of people started complaining and this is when the Tea party movement came up. A conservative group of people who wanted to see the government focus on national issues rather than focus on international conflicts. The media was able to totally discredit the movement and the points of concern these people were making, but these were the real average Americans. They understood their country is going into the wrong direction. Since the mainline Club Bush among the republicans counted these people on their side, within these people the dissatisfaction with Washington DC grew. People didn't care which party is in charge. They just wanted to be taken serious.

Then in 2006 Barack Obama appeared during the Democrat primaries. Was he the next president or just another Jesse Jackson? He was sharp, he was convincing. What a lot of people seem to have forgotten. It was Obama who promised "change". He said he will go to Washington DC and change the structure. Make politics more transparent. He said he will go and clean up the mess. It's interesting, because Obama was the first who promised to "drain the swamp" as Donald Trump later during his campaigns boasted. Obama basically said the exact same things.

Obama would then travel all over the world to give speeches. So not only Americans, almost the entire world was fascinated by this man. A person who has the potential to be the first black president of the United States. A person who could end the ridiculous wars, which were leading nowhere. A lot of people put all their hopes in it. He was basically the embodiment of what people have been looking for, for many decades. Then Obama was beating out Hillary Clinton during the primaries. He was nominated the official candidate. Since George W. Bush was no longer allowed to run, the Republicans put Senator John Mc Cain into the seat of their party. A very bad move, because Mc Cain was part of the Washington establishment and this move alienated the people who supported the tea party movement. Actually there was nothing too special about the tea party. It just helped to put an even deeper rift between the people. Somebody who watched Fox News would then become considered a right winger or tea party member. If was very un-cool to be patriotic about your own country. So here came Obama. He was basically saying what everybody was hoping for. People were tired of what was going on in the District of Columbia behind closed doors. And what John Kerry would not be able to fix, what Hillary Clinton, because she is part of the Washington elite would not be able to deliver, everybody was hoping Obama would do. I would argue here that people from both parties voted for Obama. People of all colors. It just made sense for everybody to give the outsider a chance. Everybody was ready to see the change. For African Americans and for black people all over the world a dream came true, when Obama won the presidency. Finally not only did a black person win. Also a person who everybody very obviously saw as the better candidate. I remember when I was watching the inauguration speech on my screen. I was feeling very proud and accomplished. Not only was Obama black. He was also of mixed race like I was. I hoped that this could be the beginning of a new era, where black people could finally prove to the world with the right person in charge the whole community would just take off and progress. A lot of the obstacles which we believed, stem from the wrong people in power. This could be worked on and when this man gets his second term. Black America would become a solid backbone of the American society. There seemed no limits in sight for progress to happen. Also on the African side there was a lot of hope, when Obama came to power. Would America treat Africa more serious as a business partner? Would there be ways that Africa can profit from a black president? These are simple questions, but everybody was hoping to get positive answers for these.

What we all knew of course it would not be easy for Obama. So there was a big tolerance towards his performance.

Just as the elections were over the markets crashed and before Obama started his term, George W. Bush handed the office to him with an empty cashier. A rough landing.

Still everybody already thought something like this was very likely happen. We all knew they will not leave him the office without giving him a huge problem to fix. Obama started with presenting ways how he offers more transparency. How he modernizes old structures. But 100days into his presidency not much happened. 1 year into his presidency not much happened. The wars were not ending, they were extended. All of a sudden all the funds which were supposed to help national interests were spent on new war technology. The before quite anti war Obama acted as if he cannot stop these things, but by his second term it was clear, he never really intended to stop the wars Bush had started. On the contrary, he expanded them. He then started attacks against Libya. A country which has never attacked any other country. He bombed Libya from a wealthy North African country back to the state of a backwards Muslim country. Instead of helping Africa to progress he helped to give the Saudis access to the continent. A lot of people still don't realized which role Qaddafi played in African politics. Sure he was not perfect, but he helped to keep the Arabic influence at bay. Therefore Muslim extremist groups would not have the chance to get weapons and money transferred to them. This is where we had to realize his critics were right. Barack Hussein Obama was born into a Sunni Muslim family. From his family background he was never on the side of the Africans. He was rather an ally to the Saudis. He basically helped them to change the regimes in Egypt, Tunisia and other Muslim countries during the Arab spring revolutions. These revolutions did not result into more freedom for the people. The opposite happened and most of those countries which experienced regime change became far more extremist and conservative than before the revolution.

Then when I saw what happened in Syria. The problem is that most Americans don't know people from Syria personally. Because of the Assad regime, fanatic Islam never played a big role in the country's politics. Syria had a well educated upper class. In the Middle East it was one of the more modern countries. And again they were not associated much with the Saudi Arabians. Syria negotiated with whoever they wanted. They had their ties with Russia and China, as well with Iran. President Assad was of course as any other president in the Middle East a strict ruler. A ruler without a strong grip would not be able to keep their power for long.

Assad by no means was a supporter of terror. Again here Obama supported the Islamic State in the war against Assad. Then Assad was accused to be using bio weapons against his own people, so that Obama had a reason to directly attack.

By following Obama's politics within the 8 years he was in power. There was nothing left of the Barack Obama we have seen during his campaigns. Instead of bringing "change' and "hope" to the world. He turned his two terms into a third and fourth term for George W. Bush. It looked   as if the Bushes just hired a black manager to continue with what they had started.

And this is just what has been going on outside of the United States.

Within America Obama has done nothing to encourage black people to do better. Instead he was busy inviting all these Athletes and Musicians into the white house who have been responsible for dumbing down their audience.

He paraded Jay-Z, a rapper who claims on all his records that it is necessary to sell drugs before being able to have a record deal. He kept praising all those people who have done nothing to uplift black people and he did nothing to support black scientists, black authors and the many musicians who are actively helping their communities.

Obama has totally failed when it came to ending crime in the highest populated areas of black America. He did not renew the infrastructure in those places. He was responsible that more jobs were shifted abroad rather than benefiting black people. Here it was Donald Trump who really brought those changes Obama failed to come up with. Trump started what he called opportunity zones. Places where companies would be able to hire black workers for a tax reduction. Instead of hearing Indian people talk in call centers when calling government phone lines, the call would be processed in such an opportunity zone. People would have expected Obama to come forward with ideas like this. Whenever any black issues came up Obama seemed to dodge these by showing that he is facing strong opposition by white people. Claiming Republicans blocked his efforts. Strangely there were no attempts to block his efforts for gay rights. Obama's real focus. Arguably Obama did nothing to help improving the back community, but he was the president who catered the most ever to the LGBTQ community in history. There is nothing wrong with doing this. But when looking at where the problems are, the problems with the LGTBQ community are almost nonexistent. The black community has been facing serious issues. Just to recap, the police violence towards black people. Here the black people are not totally innocent (see the chapter the black Indian paradox). Still an address by the president towards the situation could have solved the problem. I think he should have told African Americans to think first, before letting a situation escalate. What we heard from him was nothing but silence. He could have made statements that unite the country. None of such attempts were made by him. I am very sure, that most white people who have voted for Obama were the same people who later voted for Trump. I think that these people were upset with the way politics are going in Washington DC. They were ready to vote for any outsider who would offer them a recipe for change. The same people were tired of all kinds of racial tension. It's not just black people who are tired of race issues. White people want these things to be put to an end as well. The white people who are around are not the lost members of the KKK. They are the generations of the 70s and 80s. Most of them have never had any problems being around black people. I think with Obama's presidency a big chance was lost for the healing of a nation. A way to prove that diversity indeed is a strength, not a weakness. That America has had its ills and went through a long period of injustice, but finally the dream of Dr. King has won. These things could have been said. It just never happened.

I think the reason Obama was in power was the same as why

all kinds of corporations will nominate an Indian CEO as a face for their companies. You need to hire a liar who does not turn red once they are starting to fabricate all kinds of fairytales. Or just offer speeches without any meaning.

When Alex Jones published his video "The Obama Deception" on YouTube. I was reluctant to watch it. I thought Alex Jones might still dream about white superiority. So I totally dismissed it for at least a year. Then when Obama started one war after another I felt I have to watch this.

I might not agree with everything shown in there. After I then really watched it full length I cam e to the conclusion, for the main part I think people should have watched this. There were a lot of questions nobody dared to ask, because of Obama's racial status.

Nobody wanted to be shamed as a racist. Still this video was very informative and well investigated. It showed that Mr. Barack Hussein Obama was indeed part of what Trump later called the Swamp. It was no wonder that he continued on the same path his predecessor George W Bush set for him. That there are in fact many blank parts in his biography that do not add up. This guy did not apply for a job at Walmart. His job was the president of the United States. And he was the one who

pushed for more openness and more transparency. Of course
not including himself.

That Obama has two faces became very obvious to me when he
visited China. That time he held a press conference with then
President Hu and the vice president Wen. During that meeting,
Obama dared to call the two men suppressors of personal
freedom with regards to the censorship China was undertaking.
I am sure he knew that the then leaders of China were the
reformers in the communist party. Obama's attack came at the
wrong time. It gave more strength to the authoritarians in their
ranks. Especially when Obama first criticized and made the
reformers lose face, then went behind the scenes to explore
various techniques the party uses for surveillance and filtering
content online.

Over 10 years later it all makes sense when seeing how the
Biden regime and Obama's own shadow government during
the end of Trump's presidency started imposing censorship on
various platforms. I was always disturbed about how obvious
the censorship is going on here in China. On the other hand
there are enough ways to pay your way out of this. I was very
jealous of the freedoms people have when using the internet in

other countries. Whenever I visited Hong Kong, India or USA. This used to be like a breath of fresh air for me.

Now after I have been cancelled out from Linked in, YouTube and Google, China's censorship even looks a lot less aggressive to me.

I still think having a black president was important. It does not matter who he was and what he did. More important was to see that it is possible for a person of color to be able to become a president. Also very important was that there was not much racism from the people of other races towards a black president. Most people welcomed Obama and there was no extreme hatred of any kind. I think this showed that people are far less racist than the media tries to imply. Of course nobody wants to be on the bottom of society, but I cannot see huge waves of racism here at all. I really wish both sides would have used this chance. White people as well as black people. Especially for black people to clean their own act up. To finally stop finding excuses why it is OK that black on black homicide kills hundreds every months, but then start rioting when a white policeman kills a black man. Now especially with the rise of BLM activists the whole spectrum turned towards even black people to think different. While some people who are ideologically black don't see anything wrong with them. Other more open minded black people see that there must be others pulling the strings behind the curtain. More people are waking up. But to speak out in public is still not very popular with most of them.

Why I Decided To Stop Thinking About Racism

*- Chapter 7: **How Moving To China Changed Me***

I left Germany for good in 2007. I knew it was a chance that I would not get again in life. I went to Shanghai on a quick trip in April 2006. I saw the dynamic and how quick things were moving in China. I knew this was the future and left everything behind.

What I was also able to leave behind was all that psychological baggage which I have accumulated and carried around with me over the time. This was not little. My run-ins with police. The struggles I had with all kinds of government institutions, especially with the tax bureau. The growing number of jealous people who were on one hand fascinated by the moves I made, on the other it made themselves look bad, because they had similar ambitions, I was just always one step ahead. It was a real tough competition.

Also things were not going that well in Germany. The market situation was bad. The trends were changing, the overall outlook did not show a promising future. In China on the other hand, I could see a booming economy. I could see a movement towards opening up. And what I probably valued most. A great appreciation for capitalism. Meanwhile in Europe, the clocks were turning into the direction of more socialism. Socialism and Marxism have always been very popular with the younger generation. Especially those who profited from capitalism in their parent's generation and while growing up in upper classes lala land, they would gravitate towards socialism and communism. On the outside it sounds so much more humane. They totally ignore that any communist regime has always resorted in violence once they came to power.

In China at the same time the young generation was the opposite. They saw what the western countries have been able to achieve by being hard working and well educated, so the Chinese young generation thought this is something we should also do. I was able to resonate with that and here I came. Ready to start all over.

I didn't come without any contacts. My former agent in China, who is now my wife, and I started our own agency for clothing manufacturing. I did not bring many resources from Germany other than my knowledge I had for design and fashion. So the start was a complete start. It also took me 3 years to be able to understand the language. I had to start with few projects before we were able to handle the bigger ones. A lot of challenges came across my way.

just something was totally different. The excuse that some evil white man is holding me back was missing. I was all by myself. I had to rebrand myself. I was no longer the black guy struggling. And honestly it totally confused me. The people in China were so friendly. Even government offices and public services. They were all treating me like a king. I wondered if they treat everybody like this. The answer in short. No. Most Chinese applicants in the same place would be treated differently. In Shanghai I saw when I started picking some details of the language how officials were always treating migrant workers as low class people. Although throughout China there are signboards everywhere that people should use the official language, which we in foreign countries refer to as mandarin, the people in public offices in Shanghai only speak

Shanghainese. Whoever is not fluid in their language will be treated as a second class citizen. So often at police stations or household registration offices the migrant workers will have their own separate lane. That lane would have less workers, and their processing hours would be restricted. At first I thought I would have also take the same lane as the migrant workers, but a friendly woman told me take the regular one. So wherever I went I seemed to have a special status as a foreigner. There was never any differentiation between skin colors. In China as a foreigner, you are a class of your own. I could observe slight differences in treatment towards people from other Asian countries. Especially for people from the Philippines or Vietnam.

The real conflict the Chinese always seemed to have is with Japanese people. Whenever there were political tensions the treatment for Japanese people could become hostile. I noticed it while there was an ongoing feud with Japan over the disputed islands. Japanese restaurants were set on fire. Cars of Japanese brands were burned down and mobs of Chinese people were hunting for Japanese foreigners in Shanghai. In China the Japanese are viewed as an equivalent to German Nazis in World War 2. Japan had tried to conquer China and if the

United States did not fight back Japan, China could have become a Japanese colony.

In China the population is being remembered about these incidents by continuous TV plays about the Sino Japanese wars. Every child in China will learn about the pure evil mentality of the Japanese people. So how about Africans and black people? Black people in China are usually people who come there to study in university or businesspeople who engage in trade. At a certain point there were about 200.000 Africans living in the southern City of Guangzhou. A lot of Chinese friends always warned me to not visit Guangzhou, because there would be a lot of racial tension in that area.

When I visited Guangzhou around 2016 I could only account for the absolute opposite. The people were friendly. Everybody was interested in having conversation with Africans and black people. I made probably more friends in Guangzhou in one day than in a month in Shanghai. I saw communities of African Muslims to be very close with members of Chinese Muslim minorities. Of course trade seemed to be the most common connection between people. There were entire malls that just catered to African customers. They would have Chinese people serving African dishes. The opposite of what I would consider as in your face racism.

What I saw a lot were Africans misbehaving. Especially Nigerians. No matter in Shanghai or Beijing. For many years they were very visible in the nightlife areas. And they were selling drugs.

Every bigger club had Nigerian drug dealers waiting outside for customers. They seemed to have deals with the local police, so that they would share profits to escape being arrested. Nonetheless, there were incidents where security people would just beat Nigerians to death. They were so obviously selling drugs that the security personnel saw a chance to act tough. And this is the same with security people all over the world. There are people who just do the job so they once in a while can really beat somebody as close to death as possible.

This happened several times. Nigerians got a real bad reputation for that. What I really appreciate, the people made a distinction between Nigerians and other black people. We were not all thrown into the same basket.

I have seen black people from all over Africa doing fine here in China. Many people who work as teachers. Others as sports coaches, they all had it quite easy. The black people doing the best were those from non English speaking countries, or from

African countries that speak their own languages. Since Chinese has many similarities with African languages. Many Africans find it easier to speak the language than people from Europe or America. Most Africans though are unable to read or write. Still their oral skills bring them very far.

What I learned from my observation is how important it is to at least speak the language of the country you are moving to. In the beginning I thought being able to speak English is enough. After a short while you find yourself joining the Expat bubble. Once you join that club you will find expats who stayed in China for over a decade and can only speak a few words Chinese. Interestingly they are the same kind of people who would require immigrants to their own countries to learn their language. Interestingly many of them are the people with the highest paid salaries from some of the largest overseas offices of multinational corporations.

It's interesting when you are in a group of foreigners and next to you stands the architect who built the Microsoft tower in Hangzhou. You get to know the architect of wireless communications. All that would happen in the expat bubble. The problem is the bubble bursts when you stay longer than 5 years. When your original group of contacts has left and you need to get used to the younger crowds of the next wave of experts in town. All of that has its advantages and disadvantages. For myself I decided to go the opposite way. I thought about the advantages of being integrated into Chinese society. A lot of foreigners in Expat forums warned about that this would not be possible. I dare to claim the opposite. I have made many dear and valuable friendships here in China, and it is really possible.

When I am around Chinese people, they see me first of all as a foreigner. But they cannot classify me on the spot. To some people I might be American, but I don't have the NBA player type of look. To others I am African. This happens usually in summer when my skin is darker. Some people would guess I'm from India or Pakistan, since I have a pointed nose and a slim face. Some Chinese would even think I am from the western province of Xinjiang. Because I have darker skin but still speak their language. When I tell them I'm German, people always pause for a minute.

In that case over 50% will take me as German on the spot. No explanation needed. Others will ask, aren't Germans white? So I explain them that I am mixed. Then there are people who will straight ask if I'm mixed. That is usually a very small percentage. Some people are undecided, but after dealing with me for a short time they will see the traits from me that they normally associate with being German. Maybe below 1% is really familiar with global politics and will ask me if I am a refugee with a German passport. This happens maybe once in a year.

This is something what I then noticed. Once you are out of Germany, people value you very high for being German. In China the people have the biggest respect for Germans. Chinese people always tell me, Germany is as small as one Chinese province, with a population equal to one province. But you can run an economy as strong as 5 or six of our strongest provinces together.

They are very aware of that most technology in use is from Germany. All major machines, the Chinese always prefer imported from Germany. They say they have tried others, but they don't have the level of precision and planning as the Germans have. Many Chinese upper class people made shopping trips to Germany to buy German traditional products and tools from brands I have probably never heard of. So altogether when I'm in China people take me as a German who happens to be black. Wherever I go the hierarchy values me at a high level, so I have easy access to most circles.

So back to the original topic. The bad and evil white man I could blame for holding me back and the perfect excuse my personal failures no longer existed and continued to not exist. Even though when I'm in Shanghai and some German tourists would walk around and speak their language they would not think about me standing next to them in the subway that I could speak their language or even possibly come from the same place. No German would recognize me as German. It's funny because since I'm half Ghanaian. Most people from Ghana I met would somehow sense that I'm Ghanaian, even though I don't necessarily have many Ghanaian features.

What is actually interesting. In China most white people will greet other foreigners on the road, something that we Africans do probably all over the world. So I wondered why in Shanghai some random white people on the road would greet me. When I was on a forum for expats in Shanghai I got the answer. Many feel like there is some obvious racism against whites in China. They seem to have all kinds of theories of what can be interpreted as racism. So when reading their messages I thought it looks like they go through what I was feeling while I was in Germany. This again helped me to open my eyes and have a deep look at my past and realized I had two options to choose from.

Option one. I stay the way I was. I would join the club and continue thinking about race.

Option two. Take this once in a lifetime chance and turn my back on racism for good.

By reading the title you should be able to guess which choice I made.

So for me this exactly meant. I need to make peace with my past and with Mr. Whiteman.

I was very fortunate to meet some great German people while here in China. My logistics guy who took care of the China office of an international shipping company. He introduced me also to many of his friends. And also his successor, also a German, became a very good friend of mine. So After 7-8 years of being mostly around Chinese people I started my first attempts of make peace with German people. Also a big factor was my loyal customers from Germany. All of them are great entrepreneurs and I also need to credit the fashion industry for that. At the end of it the world is just one Global village.

Then another striking point I must mention here. I am, now as I am writing, 15 years gone from Germany. Gone from my hometown. And I must say, to be still in touch with many of my old friends from back home has been amazing. I cannot find the right words here. People didn't forget me over time. They always kept the contact and I have had many of my old friends coming to China for a visit. So to hell with all this talk about race. Some friends from Germany are white Germans. One of my best friends from Germany is Turkish Kurdish. I am really happy that I have been able to make great friends. It has nothing to do with the color of the skin. It has only to do with the quality of your friends.

There is another story which I must share here, because this is of great importance for me. There is this American who lived in Shanghai for a few years. I got to know him on the expat forum. He introduced himself as a black man from USA and he was quickly greeted with a lot of disrespect from other foreigners of various origins. I then wrote him personal messages and we became friends. He was into aviation and he was working at one of the major airports in Shanghai. He had a very decent position; of course he was the absolute professional in his field. He was the kind of person who did not do things halfway. He had a very serious approach towards everything he did. So one day he told me about a girl he was dating and he was quite in love. He then mentioned about how others around him would call him a Nigger. I was thinking, then answered that I never experienced that somebody called me that. I asked him if he speaks any Chinese, he said no. So this is my guess. I'm sure he misinterpreted some of the people's conversations and there are a lot of words which may sound Like "Nigger" in Chinese. So I somehow tried to explain this to him, but in his mind the Chinese seemed to be racist towards him. So the more I had to do with him the more I could see his deep underlying feeling that he judges everything coming his way as something racist. I then mentioned that I don't have the problems that he seems to have. He said it's because you are half white. Actually his skin color was the same as mine, but he had more striking African features. I then argued that my friend from Haiti is much darker than both of us and he doesn't seem to have the same problems as he complains about. He still insisted that we are much whiter in our actions. Then I saw how deeply rooted racism played a part of his entire value system. Whenever something was not his skin color he would meet it with a great level of hesitance. I felt very sorry for him. He was a great person. Very highly skilled and educated, but he never overcame the scars of his past. I don't know what exactly happened to him. I wish he could one day heal these wounds. He later moved to Africa and still spent most of his time complaining online about the racism in USA. Even his stay in Rwanda would have been a chance to heal this situation. It's just like some people can be approached with a helping hand, but their ideology would let them refuse the help.

Of course not everything is perfect in China. There are certain situations which could easily escalate. This is called Mob mentality. Whenever I would get in trouble, maybe in a factory where a boss has been messing up the goods we have produced in his factory. Once there is a loud debate starting it would attract a lot of people. In this case the people will watch the two arguing parties and start siding with one of them. So once words are being exchanged and I say something which could be interpreted as an insult to china as a country or Chinese people. The people will go wild. Like I mentioned earlier, when they started looting Japanese stores while the island dispute scenario was on the news. This can also happen in any other kind of situation.

In such cases the foreigner is in the position of the evil invader. The people bond together and do anything stupid to show their loyalty. Still this has nothing to do with race. It's a them vs. us scenario. In this case it does not matter how the foreigner looks, where he is from or what clothes he wears. Some very stupid people know this and will use it once they get into trouble.

I advise everybody who is a foreigner in China to be careful of such circumstances.

Why I Decided To Stop Thinking About Racism

- *Chapter 8: **The Law Of Attraction***

This is a rather short chapter but super important.

I by no means try to whitewash anything or compromise my own speech.

Whatever we are told by the media about racism and woke culture is completely wrong.

As hard it may sound. Parts of racial bias and even xenophobia are part of human nature.

We have become so detached with reality that we are allowing people to make absurdities become science.

A simple example. When we are in nature. We could fall prey to dangerous animals of any kind. So when we walk through a forest. We will immediately become cautions at the slight sighting of anything moving that could be a potential attacker.

Seeing an approaching bear too late could result in immediate death. The bear once hungry will see us as food. The bear could be the loveliest bear in the forest, but once the software for hunger starts in his brain, the bear will be controlled by instinct. For the victim of the bear there is no chance escaping. We humans on the other side will also have such instincts working in our brain. You don't believe me? The moment you will have a snake in front of your eyes, you will notice how you immediately develop goose bumps. These are instincts. These are programs still running in our system from the millions of years we had on our way to become the humans that we are.

Some people will be triggered by spiders, others by cockroaches. Aside from those animals you have spent a lot of time with, your acceptance for any other species will be very low.

So we humans have these mechanisms not only towards other animals. We have it once we touch cold water. Once we get into any situation which might put a threat to our lives.

With some people these instincts are stronger, with others a lot weaker. We must also understand, nobody has been able to totally switch these off. Strangely this is what the media and modern society tell us to do. It is mission impossible.

What is possible is to get used to people. We will feel better among people who resemble people who we value a lot or people that we love.

When talking to somebody who shares a lot of features with my brother I feel a lot safer.

Since I trust my brother, I subconsciously associate that other person also with people I register as safe. This is how we make our preferences. Or should we call them prejudices? Isn't this the same? Without proper judgment the chance that I get myself in trouble is very high.

Another example. I go to a neighborhood where most of the people speak another language. If I walk around with a bullion of gold in my hand in a place where the average income is super low. You don't even need to guess how long it takes until I get robbed. These are safety measures due to our common sense protocol. Not even every prejudice is based in instincts. This would be the example of using logic. The same logic women would use when a man appears in the women's washroom. The man would be seen as an intruder. The women will use instincts and defense mechanism to get rid of the problem ASAP.

When a man stands in front of you with a gun, of course you would react one way or another.

So now we have the same media, which bombards us with bloodthirsty Muslim terrorists. With gun toting gangster rappers, with characters of villains in movies, we wouldn't want to meet at night. And after showing us these they expect us to be tolerant with everybody? The media scares the people who sneeze in an elevator. As if the person sneezes everybody gets infected with a deadly virus. But at the same time you are transphobic?

All of this makes no sense at all. There are reasons to why people are careful. Some people are also aggressive at anything they do not understand. It's not the best way of dealing with problems, but unless they are not taught a better way to deal with such problems, this is their solution.

I used to be very homophobic until one of my best friends shared with me that he is gay.

This changed my perspective. I have known him for many years and we shared many experiences. So should I throw all this away because of one information he revealed about himself? He didn't harm anybody so my answer here is no.

We all have our own value systems. These grow with the

experiences we make. Some information we can be taught. Still there are things which cannot be forced upon us by authorities and we just act as if somebody changed the program in a computer.

There seem to be people in power now, who have a picture of a human in front of themselves, they can be adjusted any time by giving him or her an automated update.

It's just not how the world works. In nature there are of course different levels of tolerance. Just keep in mind. It's the very tolerant animals who will be killed by the predators first.

Once a snake makes it into a flock of rabbits, the rabbits need to run. The one who feels like cuddling with the snake will become the snake's lunch.

We are even living in a world where small mistakes have even more diverse consequences.

In our society, on the part of the governments and in their laws, there is no tolerance for crossing red lights, or filing your taxes late, or not showing up in court.

You will face the full brutality of the law immediately. There is no tolerance shown with fines or sentences. The judge raps the gavel and that's it.

So the same system wants to tell the people to be more tolerant.

The system which does not know tolerance of any kind? It's insane.

So here we are. We are told prejudices are evil, especially when white people have them.

When black people have them it's called they are dissatisfied with social injustice.

So this would be the prejudice part. Then it goes further into dating.

When you have preferences, isn't that also racist? There was a time I would feel annoyed when a girl would reject me. I would label girls rejecting me as racist. I would think the only reason would be that I'm different from others.

In this case I was right and wrong. Both at the same time. First of all a majority just doesn't want trouble. They want a boyfriend who they can imagine a relationship with. Not a boy who they cannot bring home. They would immediately get into an argument with their parents and at the same time the boy is not popular with their circle of friends. These are all social factors. So of course if they liked me, they would still think about the other factors. So I being an outsider alone diminished my chances of getting in touch with the girls I liked. Once I understood these things better I didn't face rejection anymore. So on the other hand I have my own preferences as well. Is that racist? I'm not lying when I say I always had a preference for Asian girls. It started the time I was a kid and my mother invited her friend over, who had half Pilipino daughters. I might have not shown it while they were in our place, but something inside of me was fascinated. Then later when watching martial arts movies it materialized in front of me. My favorite girls were all Asian. Especially Chinese or Japanese. So this is why most of my girlfriends were Asian. So when looking at this. Shouldn't people call me a racist, because I have my personal preferences? I had a couple of German girlfriends too. But no matter how much I liked them I would have left them for any Asian girl. Same with the black girlfriends I had. So isn't this racist?

If a white guy would clearly say in his dating profile, whites only. Hell would break loose and everybody would call him out for being a racist. But isn't the person not just honest? Doesn't he save all those non white girls from hardship? He seems to know what he wants. Maybe he is straight looking for a serious relationship and directly wants to achieve his goal without playing around? It seems like there are two sides on this coin. I might have broken a lot of hearts when playing with girls I would never get married to. So then let's throw in the homophobic angle.

Surely there are many gay people. But let's not over dramatize it. Gay people are highest 2-5% of the society. And even among those who come out as gay, half of them will later still go back to a heterosexual lifestyle. So what we learn in the media is that we must be tolerant with gay people. I think most people have no problem with gay people living their life. Enjoying the company of other gay people. There are people who feel disgusted by gay people. Also this has its justification. Here again the people have never had gay friends, have never been around gay people. For them it's the same as if a cockroach comes out from their sandwich. This is usually something that younger people express. Once people get older they will have met a handful of gay people and they make peace with that. But we all need to keep in mind. There is something about everybody, that somebody else might find lovable or disgusting. It's still based on what we find attractive/unattractive. Somebody might find a tanned body delicious. While somebody else finds it totally distasteful. In this case also culture might play a role. People in cold countries are more likely to enjoy sunbathing. But tell somebody from

Hong Kong a tan looks sexy. They will not understand it. They will only go to a beach when it's cloudy. In China it would be about class. In Hong Kong where class is not that important, people just prefer to be white. They will not hate others for having dark skin, but for themselves this is their preference. Of course as always there are exceptions.

So when a gay man approaches me and I push him back, I might need to fear to be called out a homophobe. Actually this is something which happened to me many times. I seem to be looking quite attractive to many gay men, so it happened many times that I was approached by someone. If it were in a civilized manner I would have probably never said anything bad about gay people. But in many of those cases, the gay man straight touched me without asking, so I couldn't do anything but flee. Rape is also something many gay men think is quite OK, as long as it satisfies their sex drive. There are also plenty of examples of gay family members touching young boys before puberty. This is something young heterosexual boys see as a threat. And it should not be shamed as homophobic behavior.

The examples I write here are not a statement against gay people. Like I said one of my best friends is gay. I have lesbian friends. And I have been doing events in a club which was partly an LGBT establishment. I am also in the fashion industry. Gay people are a big part of the fashion world which I would not want to miss. Still I must say honest and clear. My preference is not dating gay men. It will never be. So right now we face the early sexualizing of children. The parents will declare them as gender fluid when there are still at a toddler's age. It makes no sense. Children before they hit puberty have no sexual desires whatsoever. There are some who get into puberty earlier. But the yardstick is the puberty age. This is when the hormones develop and we humans discover our sexuality. Anybody with a sane mind should not bother kids before puberty with any sexual content. It just crates damage in their development. We are already living in a world where ½ half of most populations are on prescriptions drugs to cure their depression and mood disorders. There might be a reason why this happens. This doesn't stem from people lacking an adequate dose of pills. This might be a wet dream for the pharma industry. Not for the rest of us.

I think whatever I said about gay people also goes for transsexuals. And the same here. Before puberty also nobody should think about hormonal gender therapy. Just because these things are available does not mean they should be used. After puberty there is enough time for the child to develop its own personality and then they can decide whatever they want to do. Not just because of a fashion some athletes and superstars have been pushing.

Then to get deeper into understanding rejection. This is something we should learn about more.

In life we are very likely to face rejection. Same here, the state does it all the time. Your petition is being rejected. You appeal in court is being rejected. Your license has been terminated without appeal. These are all things which sound very common. The state is allowed to orchestrate the harshest acts of rejection, while in our social life, embarrassment seems to be something we must avoid at all cost.

Face facts, in life we face rejection all the time. If I want to play basketball in the national team. I am for sure being rejected. The clear reason is. I am too small for basketball and I don't have the necessary skills. If I decide to drive a car totally drunk and I'm killing someone. I am certain to go to prison. So these are all causalities. If I want to attract somebody I dress fine and I show my best sides instead of my worst manners. So let's say I'm a transvestite. I should understand that I'm not just exotic. I am also representing less than 0.1% of the total population. This means the majority will not have any use for me. The dating pool for casual sex might be large, but for people who are looking for starting a family I would appear totally useless. These are facts a transsexual person will have to deal with. I also know many transsexual people. Same as for humans in general, it's a matter of their personal qualities.

I think when it comes to these topics, race, gender and sexual preference. The media brainwash makes it too easy. They just declare everything as either good or evil. It's nothing different from what all religions did before them. If every channel shows something as good, we all need to behave as shown on TV. If it's shown as evil, we should object to leave it alone as far as possible. We are told to totally ignore our natural senses. Evil racist, evil bigot, evil homophobe. This list can become endless. Whoever the politics are not in favor of, can be added to the lists. It's no difference of what we saw in the Third Reich during the Nazi regime. On the list were, Jews, gypsies, handicapped, gays and Russians. For all these matters the state and the media should simply not get involved at all. It's not their business. Same goes for race. Regulations do not help anybody; it just widens the gap between sides which already don't get along.

In conclusion. Everybody has their own taste. Everybody has their own preferences. As long as nobody does anything harmful, they should be able to do whatever they want.

Why I Decided To Stop Thinking About Racism

- Chapter 9: ***The Media Influence***

---

there is no doubt that the media plays a big part in programming people's opinions.

I am for example a part of a generation which was mainly educated by TV. We did not care about what we learned in school, but we were basically trained by TV. Our style and taste were heavily influenced by Saturday morning cartoons. We were all excited about the TV shows everybody was watching. Even though we didn't have that many channels on TV during the 80s, there was so much stuff we were all watching. You had to watch Knight Rider to join the conversation in school. It was a must. Everybody was playing with He-man action figures, so the He-man TV show was a must. We all had our favorite characters, but it was really not about race or anything of that nature. We just made a pick. I'm the good guy so the other would be the bad guy. Very simple. I remember there was the black guy in then Masters of the universe action figures called "Jitsu". There was no special connection from my side just because the character was black. I used to collect all types of comic books. I had the largest comic book collections of all our friends. The same thing here. I was a fan of Spiderman and Wolverine. Because they were cool. The Teenage Mutant Ninja Turtles were just cool. That's why I liked them.

I remember there was a Shaka Zulu TV show on one of the channels. I was watching the show with my classmate who used to bully me all the time. At that point we didn't have any special discussions about the show; it was just another TV show.

Then there was "Roots" on TV. I didn't watch it myself, but I remember how my grandmother and other family members were somehow feeling emotional about it. But that seemed to last a few days. With the time there were more and more movies coming out dealing with racial topics over and over again. And there seemed to be an entire black genre about comedy.

What we didn't understand in Germany was the difference in language. We watched the Bill Cosby show all translated into German. Just later when I watched several episodes in English I found out that people would use a lot of African American slang in these.

Everything else used to be a matter of taste. There was no bias that somebody would not watch "Roseanne" because she is white or "Bill Cosby" because it's said to be for blacks only.

Then with the growth of Hip hop a lot of that changed. This change in our surrounding did not start with black people. It was that the cool white kids would only watch black TV shows. It was not cool to watch Beverly Hills 90210 anymore. We would watch the Fresh Prince and switch to something else when 90210 came on. Secretly we still watched one or two episodes, but didn't let anybody else know. We would watch a romantic movie only if that would be stuff we would be able to invite a girl to. Otherwise it was a don't. We would then watch Spike Lee movies. Because those were promoted on Yo! MTV Raps. MTV Raps was our main medium. We had a shop in town that had Vibe magazine or word up available. We were too cool to buy so whenever we saw those we stole them. So stealing magazines was cool. My friends were into baseball.

This was just Elmshorn city at that time. We didn't like

anything which was typically German. We considered

ourselves maybe the lost republic of America. This was our

thinking. So our style we got from watching Yo Raps or Rap

Pages magazine. We tried to use as many English words in our

vocabulary so we could be considered real. Our jeans had to be

Baggy, You shoes had to be the latest Basketball shoes. Best if

they were Jordans. You had to have the cool haircut. And if

you were really on point you had a gun in your pocket. At least

a replica with signal ammunition.

Our hobbies changed from regular stuff to doing graffiti.

Everybody tried to do Break dancing or Skateboarding.

Whoever did well just stuck to it. We were that tike the first

generation of young Hip hop guys in our town. But we were

very picky to be as authentic as possible. It was a style war.

Nobody was ready to lose it. I had the potential to be the most

authentic, because I had the same skin color, hair and

everything that was needed to be looking like the rappers as the

people saw them on TV. So I took this opportunity to be what

everybody else couldn't be. Still what we didn't understand

that it was all programmed by the Industry. We thought we

were rebels.

So when looking at the history of music. From the 1920s, when jazz music emerged, Black Music has always been around and it has always been popular. That was just 3 decades after slavery ended and at the end of World War 1. First of all it were black dance bars, where Alcohol was still served during the probation era, Then it expanded into swing. It attracted a lot of the richer people and then drifted apart. Then after World War 2 Rock n Roll emerged. Most of the times just after the war, the black soldiers have received their pay, so it all went as payment for the tithes to the churches. Those then bought brand new instruments. As always in the church they have a band, who then begin to experiment with the sounds and start creating their own music. This is how Rock n Roll started, Then Blues, Later in the 70s Disco. Simultaneously there was an evolution of singing and also in the musical equipment. We all know how Rock n Roll was taken from the black people by the industry. As a consequence of that, black people rightfully started their own labels. It was the quality of their music that again attracted people from all over the world and so again the music corporations went in and tried to get their hold on the music. This development peaked during the disco era in the late 70s, when black people's music reached every corners of the planet. There was a huge campaign to suppress disco music in 1983, when media companies used their influence when they labeled disco as gay. But very well understanding that black people creating music couldn't be stopped. Right when disco ended, the commercial history of Hip hop began. While the original movement was a subculture within the disco era, limited only to the boundaries of the Bronx in New York, it caught the attention of several white people who were into art and music themselves.

Basically the movie Wildstyle was the first signal of Hip Hop culture which was sent around the world. In that movie, basically the main manager Fab 5 Freddy who managed the art form at that time, went into Manhattan to look for sponsors to pick up the total package. At that time he was riding on the early success of Grandmaster Flash. This is exactly what happened. So from Charlie Ahern who directed the piece to the German TV station which sponsored it. It then attracted people like British punk entrepreneur Malcolm McLaren and others to start their own Hip Hop music projects. This is when it went onto the airwaves of popular radio stations.

Even though there were a handful of Rap songs in the market by the Sugarhill Gang and Grandmaster Flash and the Furious Five. The world still did not get exposed to a real Hip Hop sound. The earliest version that got the pure sound was buffalo gals by Malcolm McLaren. He understood what set the music apart that he heard in the parks. The scratches and the noise which came with the break beat. At the same time Rick Rubin the then manager of the Beastie Boys must have noticed it and this drove him to forget everything else and start his own label. Not only was he able to understand the sound. He knew how to make the dynamic even more magnificent. He proved this with the debuts of Run DMC and LL Cool J. Since Rubin was well connected to the industry, his peers knew to support him. It didn't stop here. Since political music was already a big thing. The Hippies of the 70s and the punks in the 80s. Hip Hop had the potential to become another genre of its own. By that time there were already people interested in working on the politics of music. To divide the people and their tastes. There were 7-8 different kinds of Rock n Roll and the fans of each type would not talk to each other. People who were into pop music would not be able to meet with hippies. It was a huge divide. The members of each genre believed they were totally independent.

Some actually were, because the number of record labels were many more than we have now left over. Somebody with a record press would actually be able to run a label if they were located in one of the bigger cities.

Opposite of what Disco used to embody. Rap music was not very inclusive. In the beginning it was enjoyed by people of all races, but with the creation of Public Enemy it became a genre for blacks only. Public Enemy had rapper Chuck D, who was basically casted into the group because he had a voice which reminded everybody of Dr. Martin Luther King. He was able to get the attention of the poorer black people. Before Public Enemy, "The Message" b y Grandmaster Flash was the only song which directly catered to the youth in the Ghettos. All other Ram music at that time was more focused on party and entertainment. With Public Enemy the life of poor people in the so called ghetto was brought more into focus. So sooner more and more people started taking about their experience in the streets. Ice T, who was more into the art of Hip Hop and Break-dance culture in the early 80s, then started as a gangster rapper in the second half of the decade. He just copied the "Parkside Killer" tape from an unknown guy in Philadelphia. With Ice T the record industry found their vehicle. He had star qualities. So this was when the industry already started working on gang movies. People always forget. When most of the gangster Rap aired in 1988. Somebody must have started working on the projects at least 2 years earlier.

The contracts and the finances were probably executed even before that.

So it was no coincidence that by 1988 the focus was on rap as the new violent form of art. It went past Hard Rock in a minute and it really caught the people's attention. The majority of people worldwide didn't hear anything about rap music before 1988. Part reason was that was the year MTV a Sumner Redstone company went international. Music videos became more important than the song itself. The rise of Music videos was embodied by Michael Jackson's career. The late 80s were full of blockbuster action movies. Blockbuster TV shows. And with the emergence of Rap music a genre was able to also deliver action music.

My personal take here is. At that time Rock and Heavy Metal were still the Goliath type of giants in the music Industry. Rock did not lack creativity at all. My thought here is that the Rock musicians were not that easy to control. Especially when it came to creative control.

A rocker would not do product placement unless he really loved the product. But that chance was little. Even bigger was the problem to have all top rockers endorse a certain product. Maybe their choice of cigarettes or alcohol. But it stopped there. Hip-Hop on the other hand was able to deliver. Starting with Run DMC rapping about their trademark Adidas shoes. Wearing Adidas tracksuits during their concerts and videos. Public Enemy wearing the latest Nike clothing. Not hiding any labels, rather adding 2 more labels to be more into people's faces. EPMD would rap about their favorite cars before even owning them. And it was part of the art form to make anything rhyme with popular products. To test the limits of what is commercially possible, the industry built MC Hammer. A young man from Oakland California. He was not only rapping faster than all the competition. He was the blueprint of what it took to be a cool guy. Hammer was able to sell anything from Coke to Pepsi. To Starter baseball jackets and Air Jordan shoes. The industry even crated cereals for Mc Hammer and whatever kind of gimmicks they were thinking of. But it might have been somebody in the music industry, who has kept his head where it was supposed to be and put an end to this. From one day to another Hammer was declared out of fashion and Rock was back for a moment. I think here the industry feared that the artists would have too much control about their career. So the investments into Hip-Hop were frozen, and probably this was the birth to some of the best music the genre ever created.

The problem with Hammer was a single artist would have too much leverage over the product. This is something which used to work in the 50s and 60s with Elvis Presley. In the 90s this would not work the same way. And it would have also given more space to independent artists to come up. What needed to happen was an entire transformation of the music industry. This is why electronic music like techno and house got the biggest budgets in the mid 90s. I would make the claim that this was a way to change the consumer market. Get away from egocentric artists and replace them with some exchangeable DJs. The main focus on flooding the marked with cheaper mass productions. So the rockers were not able to get the same record deals again as they were used to. This made Rock music a lot more unattractive. Especially for 6 members bands who needed to share profits among themselves. Then people had so much music to listen to, they would not care about the message anymore. This development was only increased by the introduction of digital music in the form of Mp3 files. Opposite of what the industry told the consumers, the music industry did not suffer from Mp3s in the early 2000s. It was a form of reset for an industry which suffered from artists with a too strong ego.

Anybody with a great voice could record music and crate a following of millions. Before. But with digital equipment all of a sudden every local wanna be singer could publish records. So it was nothing special anymore to be an artist. This gave the labels enough space to rethink their strategies and business model. By 2010 the music genres would entirely consist of musicians who have no idea about music. No talent for anything, but a strong label with a marketing plan, that works like MC Hammer's. The musician would not own anything. The artist has no control about the music at all. It's all arranged by the labels in the back. The only way the voice is palatable to human ears is because they have sound engineers who know how to tweak the musician's voice. Never before it has been this easy for the music industry to sell their music. The share for the artists has significantly dropped. And even more easy it is now to drop an artist if he doesn't go according to the plan. With this (d)evolution in music. Managers and corporations and even think tanks have been able to shape the landscape of different groups of society. I think what happened in music. Especially the divide which was happening in the early 90s has affected society in general. The same went on for TV. It's hard to have 2 people sitting next to each other to enjoy the same TV channel. Everybody is supposed to have their own little extra. And now with mobile phones we have been drifting apart even more. In a family household you have probably 5 space aliens from entirely different galaxies living together, This makes the idea of community impossible.

Then we have had the emergence of new television stations. Most notably CNN, which started during the gulf war in the early 1990s. Before that people were used to watch news at 7pm for 1 hour a day. That was it. Then CNN came and they made people become used to 24 hours news reports.

Every other hour there would be a new detail discussed. A new expert invited and there would be breaking news for information not even worth listening to. What most people didn't understand. Instead of programming people's opinion for just 1 hour a day they added another 23. And once everybody got used to see news every minute, they started creating different angles. NBC came with a news channel. Fox had their own. And for different viewers they would create another brand. So whatever was used in the 80s to separate people by subcultures they then used to separate people by the way news were reported.

The information given was exactly the same on each of the channels. But each channel had people with a different way of reporting and catering to a different type of consumer. This way it was made impossible for the son to watch the same news with his grandfather. All of a sudden the grandson would see an evil racist in his grandfather because the station he watches has been accused of all kinds of ideologies by their rival station. This would drive a big rift through families. Certain topics can no longer be discussed. Even the family cannot agree on a place anymore where they like to go to spend their holidays. TV which then leads to divorces, because man and woman have been brainwashed differently.

All this did not happen by accident. It happened by design. All this is the cleverest level of marketing psychology. Take one big market. Divide it in many pieces then sell as many more products for each division you created. One household with one single TV does not consume as much advertising as each family member separate with a mobile phone in their hands.

When a marriage gets divorced, you create 2 more market entities out of one. When then there is more hatred sown between the family members, the bigger the chance everything will be damaged and needs to be bought new. In short it creates more growth.

On one hand the consumer must earn enough money to buy new products. On the other hand people with enough money consume too slow. The people without money are actually way better as consumers. So why not then increase the taxation on the people who earn too much so that the low uneducated class gets more money to spend quicker. People with no money are known to make bad choices. They will not look for value and longevity. They just need to get things now. They have a need to boast and brag to cover up their social status. And when you get money from the government you are less likely to develop any responsibility towards it so you just spend it as soon as it comes. The people who are behind the industry, the banks, the marketers and whoever calls themselves economists. They know what to do to increase their numbers. I am very certain whatever happened in the media and the way they influenced our lifestyles and choices were no coincidence.

A system must create winners and losers. Money must always flow and stay in circulation. Otherwise there would be a standstill.

By understanding economics, I must say I do not see race in there at all. Of course race is a tool to divide the people. But it is one tool of many. The problem with black people is they are the easiest to fall into the trap. Most of them will run for any bait that is thrown after them.

Like I said before, most black people whether in Africa or in USA are not trained into exercising long term planning. They will just go with what is current. So it is very easy to show a celebrity on TV and the product sells itself. Then after that the black consumer will always be the most vulnerable to step into traps like addiction, overdrawing credits and late payments. Not knowing how to set priorities. The main point here is the shortcut thinking. I explain this in another chapter but this is the same here. People in colder regions like Europe always had to prepare for winter when fall season came. If they didn't prepare well in fall they would not survive winter.

This is the main difference between any other race and black people. Now with social justice and before that the civil rights movement. Black people are being told that they are not their own problem. The white people are. This is why so many black militant leaders have been hired to perpetuate this very same message. The reason why you are poor is not you yourself. It's the white neighbor who happens to be a better planner. This narrative will be driven to an extent where the black person would feel entitled to go over to this white neighbor and loot their entire household. Of course the black man fears the repercussions such an action would have, so the black person would go and rob the black neighbor who still has planned better than he did. Even everybody in the black community knows the guy robbed his neighbor; everybody keeps silent, because the TV told them to not cooperate with white police. The result everybody stays poor. The richest among the blacks move into a white neighborhood. In their old neighborhood only poor people get left over. Some rich investors will buy the property for cheap. Then later step by step remodel the property. How do we call that "gentrification"? Again a word nobody understands but a new way to blame the white people for the problems they have because of the shortcut lifestyle. Usually it's the men who are eager to break the cycle as long as they are young.

This is a very sensitive topic, I still think it must be discussed.

To be sure that every generation stays as poor as possible the industry offers sponsorship to people who have been picked from then poorest areas. They will reward them with all sorts of prizes. Usually these will be athletes or musicians. A lot of the poor people would probably lose hope if they didn't know somebody from their background made it. So every once in a while somebody will be picked. This person then will become very rich. Instead of using the money for anything useful they will just live a lavish lifestyle and brag as much as possible. Show rude behavior and act as they are still part of their old neighborhood. So this leads to an avalanche of events. First the kids watch these celebrities and they believe when they can be this rude, there is no need for themselves to clean their act up. Any celebrity here who does not stick to the script will be called a sellout or an undercover white person. So for any professional athlete, 10000s of kids will fail at trying the same thing. These kids will then also not get the jobs where they would be really needed. So later immigrants from Latin America will take those jobs and still be better off, than the people in then poor communities. So when the main career does not work, they don't feel to settle for less. They ego is already too high to get work at a grocery store. This is when crime kicks in. Crime offers the perfect shortcut for everybody. Just go to the corner and sell these keys and you can get rid of your debt in a short time. Oh and do this for a bit longer you can buy a car that you always wanted. Why do you want that car in the first place? Because the athlete, who came from your neighborhood advertised it. Oh and I can drink the wine that he also advertises. Then the video game, then buy some weed. The list is long. Long story short. The first person is not the only one. This affects half of the neighborhood. So the cake is not big enough for everybody to share. So competition is developing. While in any regular business field it is the skills people are hired for and then it is the performance what keeps deciding how long their career lasts. In crime the career only last until somebody more hungry or violent enters the scene. So this month, Meech is the big player. Next month Ricky enters the scene and kills Meech, takes his position until the next person is around. The likelihood again is not much different from when everybody first started to try to become the great athlete. Out of 10000 people struggling to become rich from crime. Only a handful can make it. And even their time is limited. The chance they end up in jail or dead is higher than the chance to get rich and have a great career. This again does not stop black musicians to extra promote these kinds of lifestyles. Get Rich or Die Trying, While one gets rich, thousands die trying.

Then there is the next variable. Women. Unfortunately most black women have no idea what they are doing. They believe they know everything better. They cover all their uncertainties and lack of knowledge with a loud mouth. When the husband works in a steady job, but is not making enough money, the wife will go crazy and make her man's life become like hell. The black woman also has the habit of always spending money without thinking. And her maintenance budget is incredibly high. Of course they were told by their mother not to settle for less. So they expect the man of their dreams to meet the level of what they see on TV. Either in TV dramas or of course the athletes from the same neighborhood. So here the young boys quickly understand without money they won't have it easy to impress any women. So this again makes it easier for them to pursue a career of a shortcut rather than building a steady career. When working in a supermarket the women will only laugh at a boy. Not understanding that the Mexican coworker can use this money to feed his entire family he brought over to the US and the family back home in Mexico. But the brainwash is stronger. They see the glamour they want. They push the little man towards the wrong avenue. And he believes he must quit his job and starts a shortcut career as well. He needs a new car. So he is considering starting a career as a carjacker. Hit one works. Hit 2 works. After a month he can get his own car. Then he can bring gifts home to impress his own mother. Of course in the mind of black mothers the need for questioning things does not play a big role when the bling is brighter. So she will not leave it with that one gift and be satisfied. Instead she will demand more. At that level the boy would not be able anymore to go one step back to work a normal job. Everybody keeps pushing. They all believe they deserve to live like what they see on TV. Then one carjack fails, but girlfriend is already pregnant. The owner of the car did not give in and caught the boy at his attempt to steal the car. Then the boy will immediately be brought to prison. The result is the girlfriend will become a single mother at a too young age. And the cycle will repeat with her kids. Meanwhile the Mexicans who took a regular job were able to send their kids to school and they now moved to a bigger house outside of the poor area.

The best way for the industry is to brainwash women with unrealistic expectations. This is the reason why Oprah is on TV.

This is the reason why every African American show tries to be as glamorous as possible. It is all created by design. Not because the creators are racists. They are smart business people and they do not care about people. If the people on the bottom of society were all white, they would do the exact same thing. Why they hire black athletes and actors? Because this system works forever and as long as the wheel is not broken there is no need for them to fix it. To keep the black woman in their position. There are all kinds of welfare to make sure that the women rather gets divorced than settling for less. Whenever the man does not deliver, there is the government that will pay for her. So he should better deliver.

They will not understand that the government became the husband for all the women instead.

They also don't understand that it will not be beneficial for their own children at all. Again, here is the shortcut thinking. If they themselves cannot become like the superstars. Their children will maybe make it. This is what keeps them going. The ability to self reflect is not given. And to see the bigger picture black women would need to gain the ability to have a long term view. Instead they are being fed feminism by the media, which only makes things worse.

The result is becoming an endless road of victim culture. Anybody is guilty of my misery other than myself. Then put god and religion into the equation. Oh, I already prayed, so god will do his work. Then we have the vultures. Civil rights leaders, who just encourage these people to go on as if nothing is wrong. The people in the black community do not see that the civil rights leader is nothing else but a corporate sponsored liquidation manager.

They all know about the state of the society, but these are removed enough from these areas. They know they can make it out of the neighborhood, and they understand that white women are a lot less headache than black women. Nobody wonders why the activist is never married to any local woman. The keep stressing the wealth disparity between white and black. They are giving people hope for reparations, which again would not make any sense. Wealth cannot be built on a bottomless pit. Just to see this is not yet the tipping of the iceberg. There is black media. Or black propaganda media. They will show and parade all the athletes. They will never show a black supermarket owner or a black owner of a cleaning company. It will be the musician and the athlete only. The black scientist is only available on the channels white folks watch so they see their tax dollars at least brought out somebody. There will be no engineers on BET.

Maybe on the Atlanta black star. But also for propaganda reasons only, so that black people who care, believe there is actually progress going on. Unfortunately most stories they are showing are fabricated. The black geniuses they present mostly don't exist. Still this is a good way to tease the more successful black people's egos and of course there is always the hint showing that white people try to suppress this information. So the spiral continues.

The more successful black families will usually be able to maintain their position through very hard work and very strict rules. It's no coincidence that the father is usually an Army veteran, who does anything to have his house in order. These people will do their best to try to shield their kids from the mess that is going on in the poor neighborhood. They will send their kids to private schools. Away from the place, otherwise known as the Ghetto. The industry understands this too and also has an easy pattern solution for these people. College. Once these kids are in high school they are on the course where their fathers like to have them. Because they are close to home. The father has the situation under control. Basically this could work as the back-story of the Bill Cosby show. Once the kids enter college they all start becoming activists. They then believe a form of socialism would help to bring more justice to the system. They use all their intelligence to help to fight for those the system left behind. At the end they will be depressed and miserable. This is the time they become susceptible to drugs, and then the career they could have is never going to happen. Unfortunately the parents believe the more expensive the college the better the results. They will keep telling the kids how much they have suffered to be able to afford to send the kids there. To be honest the kids will try anything but listen. For them it's the time to prove themselves. Prove that they can outperform their old patriarch. Outperform by opening up/ Ending strictness. They don't understand why this is exactly, when they become vulnerable.

Some of them will later end up in organizations like The Nation Of Islam and others. Here they will neither achieve the goals their parents they had in mind for them nor the goals they have set for themselves. But they will be under the illusion they are still busy fighting for their people. A lot of members of these organizations could have the potential to become professionals in almost every field. If they were able to see the

opportunity America offers from the eyes of an Indian

programmer, they would probably see their strength in the field

of IT. Then maybe motivate others to follow them to that field.

Unfortunately they cannot see that far.

Even most intelligent black people use the internet mostly from

the angle of a Social Justice Warrior. They are not seeing it as a

chance to investigate. To look into other cultures. What drives

them? What they might have in common. Are there ways to

cooperate? I even see that most African Americans do not even

see there are more than just 2 races. They also do not see what

opportunities it would bring to learn from white people. Most

white people are not closed minded. Here again we must

understand how hierarchy works. (See chapters before)

There are many white people who have great love and respect

for black people. So do many Asians have. It just never comes

to a conversation. The black person will feel ashamed to ask.

Complexes might often play a big role. The white person will

be afraid of maybe doing or saying something inappropriate.

It's very easy to use the wrong words and annoy somebody for

good. Or even worse get into a scenario of shame when others see it.

It didn't work in the schools where people of all different groups learned together. I had hopes for the internet because people are more anonymous. But again people still think with their skin color first. A big obstacle has been also customized content on pages like Facebook. Where black people are being shown an entire different experience online than white people would. I noticed that since I had nearly 30% Muslim friends on Facebook that I get more and more adverts showing references to the Quran or my Muslim friend's stories were shown more often than non Muslim friends. I could imagine that if you only have Muslim friends Facebook would create an entire different feel for you than for let's say an Irish hippie. Even this I would not value as racism. It's the way the industry makes money. Keep them separate and create more markets. Everybody will demand their special treatment and this enables more tailor made advertising. This will double the amount of companies that would be able to target this group specifically.

I strongly believe if the people would be a lot smarter and able to exercise critical thinking all this would not cause the same types of problems. To me it looks that people in the industry really understand the people in their markets too well, so this is why all this can happen. If I were the owner of Facebook I would be also happy to have such skilled analysts. I would also use the expertise of other marketing companies and exploit their findings to the maximum. If Facebook would not do it, some other company would do it. By learning about business and economics I was able to see the bigger picture. Just change the point of view. What would I do if I would be on the top of society?

Why I Decided To Stop Thinking About Racism

- *Chapter 10: **White People***

This is probably the most interesting Chapter for me. For me personally also the one, which is the most emotional one. So here I am. I am half black half white. My mother was the blackest woman you could think of. 100% African. My father was a very white German. Actually the ideal of a blond haired blue eyed German. Out of these 2 it was my mother who totally denied that racism played a major role in her life. My father on the other hand told me that this is something I would need to deal with. He was probably more of a pro black activist than many black people I have met in my life.

My father grew up in Nazi Germany. He was a young boy in the 1940s. He was able to see the events happening in World War 2 with his own eyes. This was the main reason why he valued freedom as most important throughout his whole life.

He was against tyranny and persecution he has seen during the

Hitler regime. He often told me the atrocities of the Nazis did

not only go against Jews. It were also Gypsies, handicapped

and Russians who were targeted. He by accident saw an

incident of where a woman living in a farm killed the children

of captive Russians.

This was an event which opened his eyes towards what fanatic

humans are able to do. He likewise condemned the cruelties of

fascist and communist regimes. This is where I agree with him

totally. I see no difference between a Nazi or a Communist

state. Both is based on the government using violence to form

and shape their own ideal society.

What is very important to mention about my father. Our family

even though we are Germans has been quite mixed. Our

family is originally from the Netherlands and settled in

Germany about 1000 years ago, another side moved from

Austria to northern Germany about 1500AD. We then also had

some influence from one Gypsy woman who was in our

ancestry. This is why my father and I have the same very

distinct nose. Indians and other central Asians see this as a

typical feature of their people. My father told me that this is from our Gypsy ancestry. I remember my grandmother always tried to hide it as much as possible. She knew during the Nazi time this could have used against them when it came to proving their Arian genealogy. Our family was very likely to have not only Gypsy blood. Also maybe a Jewish connection. Even the war was over since the 40s. My grandmother would still fear she needed to prove our racial purity.

My grandmother unlike my father was very pro Hitler. Even though her father resisted joining the Nazi party as the mayor of our village for some time, she as his daughter was inspired by fascism. It was her liking for accuracy. She wanted everything to be planned well. She disliked disturbances of any kind and even more hated to lose control. Her kind of thinking in my memory I always considered as the true German values. She disliked my father to get married. To always go the opposite way of what she felt is right for him. So when my father got married to my mother, there was a huge argument happening. She always told me about the efforts she made that I would never be born.

Once I was her grandson, she tried to direct me towards becoming as white as possible. Unfortunately for the second time her plan didn't work. She was also even less successful with my brother. I still see the time we had to live with her as one of the most disturbing moments in my life. She was a woman who really wasn't happy that my brother and I even existed. It got more out of hand when her damage control plan totally failed. She always wanted me to make friends with typical Germans. Her hope by doing this their personality would blend over to mine. The problem was these people were unbelievable cruel sadistic people. They saw me as a vulnerable fragile kind of person and totally took advantage of that. The boy who later became my classmate who lived in our neighborhood would use any chance to terrorize me. An example. We were 4 boys playing in the mud. So we used loam soil to throw at each other. This might make us dirty but otherwise it was unlikely to cause any harm. It was quite fun. Instead of using the mud only, the guy who was supposed to be my friend conspired with the other boys to put stones into the mud. Then attack me. I went home with many bruises and a brain concussion. If I had the choice I would have never wanted to see the guy ever again in life. But imagine this guy would be in my bedroom the next day just to insult me. My grandmother just told me that I must continue the friendship with him.

Even later when I went to secondary school. I was lucky I was not in class anymore with the Nazi from primary school. I then was in class with another sadist. Same thing! I was considerably smaller than him. This guy was already 6 foot tall at age 11. So the whole time during class he would step on my feet or just kick me at will. He knew I didn't have many friends, so I was his play ball. Some of the other boys found it funny, how easy it was for him to punch me down. Here it was the same thing. This boy's parents knew my grandmother and they were also churchgoers. My grandmother favored me to stay friends with him. 2 years later I put an end to this. And that was the time when I first made friends with totally different people. These friends who are still my friends to date were Italians, Kurds and Germans from polish or Prussian backgrounds. It totally freaked my grandmother out, when Michele my Italian friend came over. For her all hope was lost. She saw this as the end of her efforts. For me this was the key event to break loose from all those insane people who wanted control over my life. As much as I changed from this victory, it also shifted my views. I became more and more anti German. Most people around me were foreigners and half Germans. My older German friends, which I had outside of school, I started alienating them. Except for one German boy whose cousin was in primary school with me. He became me and my brother's German brother for all time. Apart from that I quite alienated German people. And if I had contact with them I put them in distance. The only Germans I allowed to come closer where those who accepted Hip-Hop culture. I used this throughout my life in secondary school and even beyond for making my choices who I want to have contact with and who I would ignore. I also made many exceptions. But only when these people gave me the necessary respect.

Since Hip-hop grew in popularity and I was the guy in town who represented Hip Hop in the most authentic way, I somehow used this as a shield. Hip-hop was a safe place for me. I would travel to New York once a year and bring back the latest style. I knew all the cool people in Hamburg in the inner city, and we were lucky that a lot of the German hip-hop started exactly from our town. The first events for northern German Hip-Hop. The show hosts for both music stations were all people we knew, because the scene was still a subculture and considerably small. I then knew that Hip-Hop culture would be the main vehicle for my entire later career and it proved itself right. I was able to make a living just from Hip-

Hop and Fashion.

So my way of thinking here is. Were all these Germans at that time racists? Or is this a trait that only white people have? A lot of propaganda might argue so. Many black activists call white people inherently evil. They call them the devil and blame them for anything going wrong in this world. This is what I also wanted to believe. In my chest were the beats of Public Enemy and Ice Cube pounding to the rhythm of the civil rights movement. I only wanted to prove myself right. Anything wrong I didn't accept. I then even sided with some more black extremists. We talked about open association with the nation of Islam. Even when I was in New York I was trying to find more extreme people, who would give me more confidence to support my mindset. I was lucky I could also see the opposite. Two very interesting examples.

When my father took me and my brother to New York for the first time we had to stay in the airport for a hearing by an immigration officer. We had to wait for one hour. In the same room were some strange Arab men chained to the chairs they were sitting on. When it was our turn, the immigration officer brought us to an immigration judge. To my surprise this was a black man. He looked at the 3 of us. He asked my father are these your children? My father said yes. The judge looked at us and said I don't believe these are your kids. They are black and you are white. My father gave him the passports and there was nothing the judge could do. It seemed like if he didn't need to go by the law, he would have given us a hard time. This was about the first time I experienced racism can go both ways. This judge really didn't like the idea of race mixing. To my surprise in the US that time racial mixes were not very common. A few years down the road it entirely changed. But in the early 90s this was a rather rare occurrence. There were light skin black people, but they rather had two light skin parents than one white and one black parent. So on a later trip to New York when I went shopping with my father, we ran into a group of people around Union Square in Manhattan. They saw us carrying bags of newly bought clothing. The group seemed to have watched us for a while. Then they stopped us. The 3 boys asked me. "Is that your white sugar daddy?" I asked them if they are serious. They then answered. "Hey. Tell your guy to also buy some stuff for us. Don't be selfish."

Then it dawned me that they couldn't imagine we are father and son. So step by step I understood that in the US people like my father were quite rare. The people automatically saw the races separately. This somehow showed me that this, what is called racism is very deeply rooted on both sides. This is when I started realizing what kind of role my father played in the bigger picture. That he was actually very brave for marrying my mother.

I was still quite convinced in my own racist theories. Still I saw myself looking at the bigger picture a lot more often.

Back in Germany my friend Ace, who was half German half Nigerian. He told me how he stayed in Nigeria for half a year. How his stay ended in a catastrophe and he had to come back to Germany. This was only shortly after I went to Ghana for the first time and had very positive experiences. The difference was. Just when Ace made it to Nigeria a riot started turning into a war. He stayed with his father, a very strict person, who did not like it when people had their own ideas. Ace and his father seemed to clash very often, and not only Ace. He told me how his brother committed suicide while he was staying there.

Ace like me was very proud to be black. But I could see that these events made him have serious doubts whether black people are always the victim. He saw the black person as the aggressor, in form of his father and also in form of soldiers who committed insane acts of violence towards other black people.

We were still very pro black guys. We both profited from Hip-Hop's still growing popularity. While I was quite safe in my career, Ace started to find his path. He later totally left the field of music, and let down his guard, when it came to racial matters. A lot of our friends didn't understand his motives to be doing this. But they probably never heard the story of what happened to him in Nigeria.

Up to date my story connects me with a lot of African Germans. The older these Afro Germans are the fewer they were. Nowadays we have a steady growing number of mixed children. It used to be the opposite for all generations before the 80s. Some of the older generations had annual meetings of an organization called the ISD "initiative for black Germans". I was never part of the group or went to any of their meetings. But I pretty much knew most of the members. Most of us somehow started a career in Hip-Hop or entertainment. So we all knew each other one way or another. Whenever there were concerts going on or showcases, there were highest 10 black people in the crowd. And we were always the same 10 people. In my town I used to be the most influential black guy. I was not the oldest. But we all knew each other. We were totally between 10-20 black people in a town of then 50.000 people. We were all somehow connected through similar stories. What I found most striking. In almost all of the cases, it would not be the black parent taking care of the children. It was always the white parent. For most of them, it was clear because they had white mothers. According to the law it's more likely that the judge will decide in favor of the mother, when it comes who will get custody over the children. I my case it was my father who took care of me and my brother. In our case, my mother suffered from schizophrenia. She became more and more religious over the years, making a marriage with my father almost impossible. Even though he has had the extreme burden on himself, my father never for one day thought about leaving me and my brother behind. We were his total pride. My mother was unable to love her children because of the brainwash she received. But there was not a moment my father was not there for us. There were times when we took this love for granted and made his life even harder. Still he didn't give up and always showed real strength.

This is why I must say it is a matter of character. It has nothing to do with the color of the skin.

It also has nothing to do with the financial resources. My father was at the verge of bankruptcy for most of his later days. He has lost everything valuable due to financial problems. He still never gave up.

People always argue that white people are privileged. That resources have been unevenly distributed. During my trips all over the world I must say, this is not the case. People go through hardships everywhere. When it comes to hard work, it's the northerners from cold climates who are most determined. They are able to exercise long term planning and therefore they have an advantage. If they would be lazy they would have died out during the winter months. You could not live in Germany or Norway and not have your harvest in by the end of fall season. My father was a farmer, so he wasn't removed from the natural cycles that long. For people from closer to the equator all this is not as serious. The amount of people that is only dreaming, day in day out, is bigger than the people who actually move something. I could see this in Africa, I could see this in India. Even in China where everybody is hard working. Still the people in northern places or form northern places are working harder and faster. Maybe not better. But there is a difference between north and south.

This is also reflected in their life choices and the way they manage wealth. The further people go south the less likely it is to find multigenerational wealth. Especially for the average person.

The way friendships are being handled is also a lot different. In my experience, if you make friends with Russians from Siberia, you have a friend for life. In other places further to the south friendships can be more superficial. Still people with existing family ties also tend to be more valuable friends. People in the north are more cold hearted. The warmth on the other hand people in warmer regions offer is also a big plus for those places. When it comes to live a life of pure joy. Nothing beats Africa. So by looking at the bigger picture, geographical aspects play a big role. Everything needs to be seen in relation to each other. And also I would not value one side more than the other. I have learned that I am actually the most fortunate by being part of all sides.

This is why I gave my book this title. I don't see any need to think about race anymore. I am proud of my white side as well as my black side. And not only this. I live in China for 15 years, my wife is Chinese and my kids will be half Chinese.

Whatever comes after me depends on my own performance in this life. I cannot use race to cover up my own imperfections. I cannot use race as an excuse for my personal failures. I even understand that in many cases I received a terrible treatment, because I was not tough enough. I then learned from these experiences how to become tough. I had to go through this school of sadists to not become one myself. I could have easily reversed what I had experienced and I could have punished other people. I never felt this kind of revenge would help. I was always looking forward to the next challenge.

Here I am. I might not be perfect. But I have high requirements for this world I'm living in.

At this point where we are bombarded with messages by governments and corporations pushing for ending racism by punishing those people who might act racist is purely wrong. Sharing my experience is probably a part of the solution.

As much as we were hoping for Muslims to make a united stance against terrorism, I am now here and make my case clear what my thinking looks like about racism.

I do not hate anybody based on their color, gender or whatever else they are born with. I let only decide if we can get along or not. The career politicians and the civil rights leaders, who are making a living from these conditions. I despise them. They create a problem in the first place. Then they offer a solution via censorship which they actually need for covering up their own failures and use racism as a vehicle. The old divide and conquer principle which we see since ancient Rome.

For the rule of the few over the many.

There will always be people who do not like a certain color. There will always be people who prefer one type of person over another. There will always be people arguing about total nonsense. People will love each other. People will hurt each other. All this is part of life.
We must learn to accept it, deal with it. Tell our loved ones to understand this. This is life.

Why I Decided To Stop Thinking About Racism

- *Chapter 11:* **Black Character Anomaly**

There was a time I was perfectly sure. The key to black people's problems was only racism from the direction of white people. The white people just hated each and any one of us. And we were just the good little sheep which have done nothing wrong, other than being ourselves a bit too much.

I had a mother who already would not support my view. She claimed to not have been exposed to racism at any point in her life. She mentioned this when I was around 20 years old. I explained this to myself that she has always been a more conservative kind of person and it is part of the reason she moved to Germany as an adult. She never had to make it through the school system. She never had to make it through our youth culture.

She came from a very privileged family in Ghana. She would never mix with poor people or people she felt were below her class. I guessed this already eliminates a large percentage of troublemakers and uneducated folks who would of course show their blatant form of racism.

Still I assumed since she is a Christian or even more strict as a Mormon. She is the person we would call Uncle Toms. Black people who would deny any negative occurrences in their lives, derived from white people. To a certain extent that was what I thought of her. On the other hand, by looking back, she has never been mistreated by anybody. She never really needed to fight for her position. She was not the only one. Many others also didn't need to struggle.

Then there came this event which opened my eyes why it is like this.

In the 80s my parents let a man from Ghana stay in our house. He was an asylum seeker. He has been seeking for political asylum in Europe and was later granted a staying permission by the German government. I refer to him as Uncle Ben. We were very close with him and his family until he decided to move back to Ghana as the political environment improved during the 90s.

In 2004 his son who was born in my hometown decided to come back to Germany.

He notified me once he would travel and then all of a sudden he was in Hamburg. So I went to pick him up and he was staying in our house.

That was the beginning of a very interesting time. Ben, who had the same name as his father, would be very enthusiastic about life in Germany. He was the person who always wished to come to Germany to pursue his career and dreams from there. I then told him very clear that it is not that easy. There will be many obstacles he has to overcome. I explained him about my own experiences with racism. For him it was so hard to believe, he completely didn't register this at all. Since he came on a normal travel visa, he only had 2 months left. So we went around and he really enjoyed the time. What I saw from the very beginning, he would be able to make friends with people I could not make friends with. People would listen to him, who would never listen to me. And especially all the girls loved him. He couldn't even save himself from the big amounts of girls chasing him. So how could that be? He was much darker than me. He didn't have any income? He was not established in the otherwise so tight knit society at all.

I really wondered. I analyzed. I studied.

So with each day I could see that it was his magnetic personality which helped him open all the doors for him. His charming attitude. He would never have negative emotions in his heart.

I had so many preconceptions of what to expect from people so that I probably always got what I expected. For him he didn't expect anything bad and also never got bad things in return. For the first 2 month it was absolutely fun. Then because he overstayed his Visa, the police was chasing him. This resulted in a long hide and seek episode with the law. One day our neighbor has notified the police when he saw him. I was quite disappointed that this neighbor did this. He as a half Chinese, married then to a Greek wife and with even Nigerian relatives in his family. I was very surprised that he was the one to call the police. I later found out that he was cheated very badly by Nigerian scammers that I guess he used this as a payback. Bad enough, this brought Ben into a tough situation with local law enforcers. Still here Ben took it with ease. One day he accidently ran into one of the policemen who arrested him before. Instead of getting angry or react with negative emotions, he would greet him and be very friendly with this policeman. I know myself how I would have reacted in his place I would probably just run. The policeman would call his colleagues and then the hunt would be on.

Ben was friendly, wished the policeman a safe trip. He said he is also moving out of the country soon and the tensions were eased for that moment. I will later dedicate a whole chapter to Ben in my next book. I just want to make the point here. This guy had the absolute amazing personality. He didn't have the same baggage on him as I did. His view of the country was very positive, so he came and almost always got what he wanted. I on the other hand had preconceptions. I believed the people were against me, so I just fulfilled my own prophecies. By studying him I really started understanding my mistakes. I just didn't change overnight. I must confess a lot what Ben was doing I soaked it up in my own personality.

Especially when I started new in China. His experiences in Germany, were the ones that helped me to start from a different angle when I came to China. I never let negativity affect me to a larger degree. I also stayed away from those who did let that happen.

Another interesting point I realized just some months before I wrote this book. I had several discussions with my friend Daniel, who is also a half German half Ghanaian, from the same area in Germany. He is 5 years older than me. He also travelled to China to see me very often and then also began doing business here. He now lives in Hong Kong. He still thinks a lot about the racism which he experienced in his past. So we would have discussions if we had children if would we send them to school in Germany?

He always stresses he would never like to let his children suffer the way he suffered. Still, I must say here, he grew up there 5 years before me. In his generation there were far less black people in Germany.

So I remembered my times in primary school. How I was being bullied. I didn't tell him, but I kept thinking about his words. Was my time in school so bad and was I hated so much because I was the only black guy? I went in depth about my experiences in school, in the previous chapter "Racism in school". In elementary school I was indeed the only black guy. But just for the first 2 years. Then my brother started in the same school. He didn't have the same problems that I had. He was well respected and feared by others because he was the one to bully everybody else.

Then looking back at our neighborhood. Were we the only

black guys? No. We weren't. The neighbor's son opposite of

my Grandmother's house was mixed, too. He was also a bit

older. Perhaps the same age as Daniel. He didn't seem to have

any problems at all. The problem was maybe. I didn't like him.

He didn't fit into my view a black guy should act like. This

neighbor would call himself "Schoko" referring to himself as

chocolate. I didn't like it when I was called nicknames of

chocolate brands or brown colored sweets. So I saw everybody

who did take those names as a sellout. I remember I never

spoke with him and never felt the need to.

Just looking back it was not him who had a problem. It was me.

The same thing happened in secondary school. While I was

back to my outsider role in school. This time forming a group

with 2 other outsider guys, I was still not the only black guy in

class. There was the other black guy Marco. He was adopted

by very religious German people. He was more of a funny guy.

He liked playing the "class clown". He was not offended when

people would call him names, he would laugh it off. He came

from a village which was much further away from town than

my place was. Because most of our classmates came from the

same village, he was already established in the group. I wasn't. Since he was better in sports, he would be a popular pick for the sports team while I wasn't. Strangely all over the years I seemed to have forgotten that there was even another black boy in class. His skin was darker than mine. With a far more striking appearance. So who am I to claim, I was the one who was held back by racism?

Marco and his brother Holger later quit our school, due to low grades. Unfortunately they both got into drugs and alcoholism very early. I still saw them once in a while, but we didn't really have close contact. Strange as the world is, I always saw them as white boys. I never realized I went to school with several other black people.

So again when I did my sophomore year, in the new class there was the daughter of my mother's best friend. A very nice black girl. Everybody seemed to love her and she was totally integrated into the group of this class. At that point the class was a very tight knit group. Everybody seemed to get along quite well. When I got into the group, I was basically on a different mindset. I was the total outsider before. I was living in gangland in my free time. And then I got into a classroom with really nice people. I somehow really screwed this up. I was so pro black brainwashed. All I had on my mind were

Public Enemy and NWA records.

Every white person was a joke to me, so I just fired shots

wherever I wanted. There was a British guy in class. I always

called him slave trader, because I just read Malcolm X.

The black girl, she was not mixed like me, but she didn't seem

to have any problems. At least not the problems I thought I had.

Her little sister also didn't seem to be in constant fight mode.

So it also proved my view of us being suppressed totally wrong.

But the brainwash was stronger.

All the cool rappers always told me that we have to fight

racism everywhere. Malcolm X was basically fighting racism

all his life. All the guys in my gang were all white people

believing to be black activists. They only motivated me to

further go into that direction. This was what made me a cool

guy. This was what made me stick out. I was the authentic

black guy like in the Hip-Hop media. Every other black person

not going with this image was an Uncle Tom type sellout to me.

This was also the time when The Fresh Prince of Bel Air aired

on TV in Germany.

Sounds quite strange why should a racial superior country show "The Fresh Prince" or the "Bill Cosby Show" on primetime spots. But, hey. I was the last to understand what cultural revolution of multimedia we were exposed to. From that time on I wanted to be Will Smith. All other black people I knew were sellouts like "Carlton Banks". This picture was so deeply anchored in my mind that it took me decades to unlearn it.

We were believing we were fighting against racism, and then we would eliminate the characters who would be great examples of black excellence for a stubborn wannabe gang member guy who has his own twisted value system of what he considers cool or authentic. The problem is. Anything this person / fool sees as authentic is not to the benefit of his own people.

My type of people saw pride in getting arrested, getting in trouble with the law. We would be proud of our drugs and alcohol. Then alienate anybody who thinks we might have a problem.

And dontcha dare to lecture us. We would rather see racism as the source of our failure than ourselves being stubborn to be the major reason. I was only lucky that I was later able to at least lift myself out of this mess and then move into a more positive direction.

What I really disliked about many characters at that time. The majority of classmates were very leftist, left leaning. I was very much against right wingers and neo Nazi fascists, since I have often been a victim of their attacks. Still I disliked the total leftist agenda. I always felt that these people were so fake at whatever they did. They were so hardly trying to fit into a strict set of rules which was sold to them as the freedom socialism is providing. Yes these people were open minded. As long as you behaved in exactly the way they expected people to behave. If you were a little off. They would begin the witch hunt. They were often very militant in expressing their disappointment. All these extreme things as cancel culture we see nowadays were already an issue back then. Hypersensitive people who believed only their own opinion can save the world. In a way I was no different. I was sensitive in my ways believing I was sort of a black activist. They on the other hand believed they were the totally open minded young generation, but you had to feel the bliss of socialism by yourself or there was no chance in fitting in. Imagine that these people nowadays are the ones who are into politics…

Why I Decided To Stop Thinking About Racism

- *Chapter 12: **The Black Indian Paradox***

The most interesting aspect of racism is which I found here.
During my trips to the US I have been looking at people from
all different backgrounds. The main topic is always about white
or black. We still need to acknowledge there are different
shades in between. So in this specific case I was looking at
Indian people. Especially south Indians.

When I travelled to USA, wherever I went. Most especially at
the airports, the largest crowds would be the Chinese and then
followed by the Indian travelers. Over the past decades. Many
well educated Indians have been seeing their chance in starting
a career in the United States. Most of them in the service sector,
with many in the field of IT.

In many well known IT companies, a large number of Indian

programmers come from the southern Indian city of Bangaluru. A city which is known for that the natural resources were scarce. In search of finding a way for them to survive, the people saw the greatest value in their education. So they have exploited their minds as their most valuable assets.

In short their intelligence is what works for them. This is something people all over the world have noticed. Firstly people from that area were hired as call center managers. Then their employers saw that many people are very skilled at mathematics and easily developed skills which were needed for programming advanced software. This may even have been viewed as a potential competitor to Silicon Valley. If the American companies would not have been tapping into that pool of resources, sooner or later there could have been Indian IT companies developing which could bring them serious competition.

With a good set of education also comes an excellent set of manners. Intelligent people are usually less aggressive in their daily life. They know how to plan their careers. It's clear that many of these people later enjoy a long term occupation. They are able to sustain their families. They are able to provide for

2-3 generations in their household. Even in very expensive places like San Francisco many will manage to even make their salaries work, so that family members later start their own businesses. It all works because these people bring structure into their lives. They took the opportunity which was offered to them and they knew what to do, to make the best out of it. Since they are from India they will have English at least as their second or third language. They will be fluent in written English and they will be able to speak the language. They might have somewhat of an Indian accent. Some will lose it after a few years others will keep it for a lifetime. Usually if the first generation becomes successful, the second generation will do their best to at least keep the level. So it is hard to find Indian Americans to be on the poorer side of society.

So now here is the main point. They came to America as immigrants. They probably lived in USA for 2-3 years. They are already surpassing most Americans of other races.

They come from a country which people would label 3rd world. Even with many programmers born into families from a background of a very poor caste. So it takes a short time for them to make it in America.

They usually have very dark skin. Some could be even darker than African Americans.

They are very visible as Indians. Anybody can see they are foreigners. Anybody can guess their country of origin must be India.

My question here is. They will go through the same police checks as black Americans pass through. They look significantly non white. They according to regular police officer's thought do not speak proper English. The officers might have a hard time conversating with them.

So let us assume there is white evilness. There are white people who really hate non white people. Let's assume the white policemen hate anybody who has different skin color than them. Anybody who might be a possible reason for white people losing their jobs. Anybody who does not fit into their pattern blueprint of a white society.

Wouldn't these people be the perfect choice of an attack by the white evildoers? Wouldn't they be glad to "whoop" an Indian person's ass? This here should be their chance.

My question is why don't we see that happening? Why aren't even southern Indians being confused with African Americans during police checks? Why don't we see an Indian Rodney King?

If there would be such hatred on the side of white people for non whites. Why don't we see an Indian George Floyd?

The question I ask myself. Is this about skin color or rather about attitude?

Let's face facts. These young southern Indian people are very motivated because of the opportunity they were given. They feel happy to be in the United States. Anything they experience they value as novelty.

Black Americans on the other hands are fueled with a negative image of white people.

News about racial tensions, violence and inequality dominate the media. Music which is ingrained with an undertone of fighting the oppressor. There is a history of segregation on half of the states. There is also the history of slavery. Black people believe they have paid their dues while their ancestors were slaves. Meanwhile a young generation of Indians, Pakistanis and also Nigerians are at their doorstep and only see the positive sides. They know back home it is far more difficult to make it up in society than in USA.

USA is a capitalist country. A place where your actions are more important than your connections. A place of a show and prove mentality. A country where hard work will lead to good fortune. A country unlike many others which for the most time of the previous century enjoyed political and financial stability. These are important factors, somebody from outside America values very much. People from inside of America have no other points of reference or experiences so it is easier for the news media industry to make them feel as if the country is not treating them well as a collective.

What is the problem here?

Actually African Americans have many advantages. Advantages that moist of them are unaware of. The main one is. They are able to speak the official language.

In the event of competition a lot of foreigners need to start from a much lower level than most African Americans do. When they enter USA they are not able to speak good English. They don't know the general etiquette. They have no connections to public services. They are not allowed to vote. They are not part of the social security system.

All these are things that African Americans have in advantage.

Then there is school education. African Americans are usually studying in public schools all over the country. They have access to great libraries and they have access to all the resources the American educational system has to offer. They might not be as new or clean as in private schools. But for most white Americans, private schools would also be too expensive to attend.

The tricky part. Everybody is attending the same type of schools in America. News and stories of budget cuts and classrooms overcrowding. De-motivated teachers and general neglect make the round. Still one needs to consider that the average public school is still 20times better equipped than current public schools in India. Over 2 decades ago the difference was even more obvious. And that is the time when the current wave of immigrants used to go to school.
The difference is. The individual's value system. The Indian

student will not value their badly equipped school as something negative. Strangely the African American Student will not pay attention to what is happening in school. The excuse will be my school is underfunded.

Why do they think like this? Is there any media in India talking about schools being underfunded? Do they constantly show drop outs as super rich celebrities?

Do they pay most of their attention on some semi illiterate athletes?

I guess the answers are always no.

Their value system is different. The same happens with the police. An African American will watch hundreds of movies, listen to thousands of albums of entertainers creating an environment of good vs. evil. Where the evil police hates black people.

Every story will show the black person as the victim only.

My take on this. And I might sound controversial.

There are many African Americans. Especially career criminals who understand that this is absolutely untrue. But they know whatever the outcome is. The narrative will be on their side.

They will absolutely be non compliant at any attempt the police is doing their work.

Some of them will even commit a crime and then challenge the police to not touch them or else they will tell the story as if they have been unjustly treated.

The "chip on my shoulder" behavior is already the norm. For the policemen the daily experience is, that once stopping the car of a black person automatically the skin color issue comes up. And I bet a lot of money. Black cops will always be called Uncle Tom. This is an omnipresent role play, destined to end up in a catastrophe. The prejudices of the policemen towards the average black person are as much as the prejudices of the black person towards the police officers.

The past of the United States is bad enough. Slavery remains a huge burden in the US society. This will not disappear too quickly. The problem is that the burden of slavery is still in the minds of African Americans. They don't see that the shackles have been removed a long time ago. This makes it so easy for other foreigners to enter the country and bypass them on the social ladder within months. It is always incredible at what speed that happens. Now many decades into this development still nothing seems to help. I would argue to fix the social problems it would be as little as picking up some books once in a while, which are not just for entertainment. And then really work on their personal work ethic. Reduce pride to a healthy level and start working. Maybe work like a slave. Maybe work for a lower salary to enter the market.

There are Mexicans with zero skills snatching all the jobs away which African Americans potentially could hold. Also nothing happening on that side.

The will to make a change is not there. The will to do some extra work will always be misunderstood as being a slave or sellout. But then when somebody does a little better there is jealousy again. Oh that guy is acting white. We all know this kind of talk.

We all know things are not as good for African Americans, but we know that the color of the skin is not the problem. The willingness to take action is. The willingness to make a change. There are people who make these adjustments and they are usually very successful. It's just like most people don't take notice. It's still less interesting than watching the latest rapper who seems to be a billionaire at age 23. People don't seem to realize that entertainment is not real. They go the easy way. Easy means, not taking any action. And in case things go wrong, blame the person who took action for your own failure.

In case black Americans would idolize an Indian coder. This is hypothetically speaking. They would probably be less emotional but have a more rational approach to answer the officer. Maybe they would be able to think from the point of view of the policeman. Treat him nice so that he can also treat you a bit nicer so that he will also like to save himself from unnecessary stress. Of course there are policemen who are behaving terrible. This does not mean that every other policeman is behaving exactly the same. So what does the average African American have to lose to educate themselves and find a way to master such situations with ease? Probably have a better handling than any other group in society has? We should look into this as one of the many possible solutions.

So my conclusion here is. This is one of the best examples that police brutality has nothing to do with race. It's a matter of class. An aggressive and super emotional white person will be in trouble with the police about the same time as a black

American.

When it comes to the law the white person will still be able to deal with it in a better way, because white people will have a plan available before such an event happens. They will know which lawyer to call. In general they are much better organized. In black culture the preparations to not escalate such an event do not happen. Only when the damage has already happened, a so called civil rights leader will show up on the spot. We should not forget. The victimhood is the main source of their business. Blaming others is the only recipe they know of getting attention for themselves. In Indian and other foreign communities such people hardly ever exist.

But one thing is certain. In case of severe violence against their own people also the Indian people will riot.

So let's look at the policemen and women.
They are not from the top level of the society. Usually most were once in the army, served some time as soldiers and then got a safe job for themselves at the local police office. Others had higher ambitions but they were not that bright and took a

police job instead. Being part of the police allows you to have an average life. You will not become rich or poor. The only piece of pride is your badge and your gun. Without that most of these officers would be psychologically naked. As confident as they look, the same level goes for their insecurities. They are on one hand the representatives of state force, on the other all that legal stuff is already too much for what is supposed to fit into their heads. Many of them have to work the late shift to make enough money to sustain their families. Many have internal pressure within the departments. So unfortunately those who are not that smart, carry a lot of baggage with them from the first encounter with people of different social classes. It sticks to their psyche when somebody they believe is supposed to be on the bottom of society and drives around in a Rolls Royce they could never afford. A simple minded person will straight get jealous. So expect the police person to become jealous. They will suggest the person must be a criminal. They will only make simple conclusions. They will think something stupid. But also don't forget. If the alleged victim would have their own emotions in order, this can be handled without any confrontation. Just be a few decibels more quiet. Show them the papers and if they still try to delay things just tell them that

you understand your laws. Nothing will happen.

Like I already said in previous chapters.

In America the social pressure is a lot.

Different groups of society are competing with each other.

Nobody wants to lose, nobody wants to give in.

So the best way to get through all this is to be less emotional.

Know the law and communicate this.

Why I Decided To Stop Thinking About Racism

- Chapter 13: ***Why I Decided...***

Why I decided to stop about racism. I have given you various examples and reasons why I believe racism is partly natural, nonexistent and totally useless. I have been doing business since I'm 16 years old. I always engaged in trade, in sales and also in planning events.

It happened to me sometimes people were surprised by my appearance, but in general. As soon as the people saw that I am very professional, there were no further problems. Anywhere I did business; it's all about being able to deliver. Somebody needs 20,000 T-shirts. Nobody cares about the skin color of the person selling those. When working on a project of half a million $. Nobody cares what color their opposite person has. What everybody cares about. Can they deliver?

And again prejudices are a great tool to analyze your opposite. Of course everybody is trying to find the error. Everybody must find the error. In case something goes wrong every person in the chain will make losses. So in business we do not discriminate by color. Or gender. We discriminate by statistics. By the person's track record. Nobody will offer somebody a 30 million construction deal if the person has never successfully executed such a project. The person who can manage such a project with ease comes first to mind. We call these people established. They are established because they are the main go to person for this issue. They are the ones who offer the best solution. They are the ones everybody would listen to when they need help as well. They are the ones while others are stuck with a problem, who will not face problems. This is the main advantage to work with an established person. So to be able to bypass this, you need to be really convincing. People who engage in business and have a track record of just a few months in a business field will not be taken serious. The only way for them to get by is take the jobs nobody else would take. Sell for a price others would not be able to sell. This is of course accompanied by hardship. But without a struggle nobody will let you take over their marketplace. Everybody has gone through the same struggle.

This also tests the personality of the individual person. Somebody who easily gives up should better apply for a regular job. Somebody who is looking for steadiness in life should better get a regular 9 to 5. The world of business is a war. You need to build a company like an army. You only want the best fitting people. This is the same for sports teams, the same for universities. Everything there is competition going on. It's basically a war. The ones who are fighting hard and the ones who are best prepared can make it. Everybody else will not do so great. Factors like race play no role here. It plays a role when entertainment tells people of a certain group; they do not need to work hard. And this is what is happening. When every girl will be told her main priority in life is to dance with the stars. Then it is no wonder when most girls will go that direction. So the fewer girls are going in the other direction, the harder it is for them to establish.

I had my fair share with this and I had more than a few hundred times the chance to blame all my troubles on white people. And even now I might still blame others for things that I personally messed up. We are all not perfect.

I still must stress that not believing in racism anymore was instrumental in my growth as a person. It was essential for my success. So many doors were able to open because I worked on my attitude. My many travels enabled me to see the bigger picture and offered me a way to understand people from different backgrounds from their own point of view.

I know what ambitions a young singer from Nepal has. What his struggles are. How strong his personality must be to make his breakthrough. Why? It's Because, I have met such a person. I have met so many great people all around the world. I had to see that having friends in every corner of the planet is like a huge treasure, especially since we are able to use modern technology to communicate. But even before the internet we were able to keep in contact. I see this as real wealth. "Tell me who your friends are and I can tell you how successful you are" is a very true statement. Still I like to inspire people. I always tell people the story of many old Gong Fu movies. The young adult joins the wuguan (dojo). He asks the shifu/master to teach him Gong Fu. Instead of learning the techniques from the beginning, the shifu will hand the man a bucket and a piece of cloth. Go clean the gym.

This is the lesson everybody must go through. There is no reason to skip the first step.

Maybe this is what we are being told by the media. Genius Xyz skipped secondary school and straight went to college. This is something which does not make sense. Sure there are some individuals who have been doing this. But it would be good if the media would tell the whole story.

In many cases these people have already been learning at home. They already have something setup which enables them to be far ahead of other students. I remember being in school with a guy who was excellent in chemistry. He very early made it to become a professor. He was able to skip classes. His knowledge of chemistry was far advanced than what the teachers were teaching us by the books. So at times he would correct the teacher or take over the class by himself. Why could he do this? Since a very young age, he was interested in chemistry. So he was not satisfied when he only had a small experimental kit, He wanted a small lab for himself. He himself went out and read all the books about chemistry in a public library. So before he finished primary school, he was already an expert in math, chemistry and physics. His speaking skills were also already advanced, since he happened to invest a considerable amount of time in reading and also writing. So at age 12 he was already at the level of somebody 2 years older than his age. If people spend a lot of time with a particular subject and their physical and mental capacity is still able to process more, then to others this person looks like a genius. I can share this because I was lucky to be around several geniuses. They are all people I greatly respect and admire. Just being around them has also helped me a lot on my path. Same case here, they all have different skin colors from me. If I would have rejected them from the beginning, I would not have been able to make these experiences. Just because I am lacking some crucial experience, I would have to resort in reading books about such people. And we all know that would not be quite the same.

I would just inspire everybody to open their eyes. My father always told me "open your eyes". "You will be able to see what others don't see". The same goes for the mind.

This is why no matter what things like racism, which is just an ideology like any other, will not bring us anywhere. Ideology further down the road becomes a religion. You want by all means to fulfill your prophecy. I remember when a Dr. Umar Johnson made a video about that all Chinese people are racist towards black people. And he is somebody people are listening to. When applying common sense one will see, this man has only one job. "Racism". He is a so called activist. His heart is full of preconceptions. By looking at him there might be a lot of people who really see the dark cloud hanging over his head. They will of course avoid him. Some people can sense negative energy. In this book I have given numerous examples how important attitude is. So I will only encourage everybody who does have reoccurring problems with racism, to go and analyze their own behavior first. Then check if really everybody around them has the exact same problem. I doubt it.

I hope I was able to inspire everybody who read this book. I understand that leaving your own pattern is not easy. But please give this a try. Whoever wants to leave me a feedback about this book. Please contact me on my website. I am already very excited hearing from you.

I wrote this book out of love for everybody. I'm trying to offer a solution, which has worked for me amazingly. So I wish everybody who reads this a great success and more happiness.

Asher Sommer